Straight Talk for Today's Teacher

Straight Talk for Today's Teacher

How to Teach so Students Learn

Adrienne Mack-Kirschner

HEINEMANN
Portsmouth, NH

Heinemann

A division of Reed Elsevier Inc.

361 Hanover Street

Portsmouth, NH 03801–3912

www.heinemann.com

Offices and agents throughout the world

Library of Congress Cataloging-in-Publication Data

Mack-Kirschner, Adrienne, 1944–

  Straight talk for today's teacher : how to teach so students learn / Adrienne Mack-Kirschner.

    p. cm.

  Includes bibliographical references and index.

  ISBN 0-325-00696-2 (alk. paper)

  1. Effective teaching. 2. Learning. 3. Teacher-student relationships. I. Title.

LB1025.3.M3344 2005

371.102—dc22   2004020534

Editor: Lois Bridges

Production: Elizabeth Valway

Cover design: Night & Day Design

Cover photo: Kelly Hancock, Monroe High School, Los Angeles and her students; photo taken by Lewis Chappealear, Monroe High School

Composition: Argosy

Manufacturing: Steve Bernier

Printed in the United States of America on acid-free paper

09 08 07 06 05 RRD 1 2 3 4 5

Dedicated to my granddaughter, Alexandria Simon.

"Kids don't want to be managed.
We want to be taught by caring teachers so we can learn."

Alexandria, age 9

Contents

Preface   ix

Acknowledgments   xi

How to Use This Book: xiii
A Friendly Instruction Manual

One   Teaching with the Brain in Mind: 1
The Brain Has a Mind of Its Own

Two   Classroom Environment: It All Begins with You   9

Three   Motivation: When Teachers Care,   30
Students Will Follow

Four   Beginning with the End in Mind: 34
A Case for Why the End Is the Beginning

Five   Assessments: Why We Do What We Do   51
and How We Can Do It Better

Six   Student Portfolios: Collect, Select, Reflect   64

Seven   Habits of Mind: Behaviors That Make   83
for Student Success

Eight   Student-Led Conferences: Letting Kids Talk   89

Nine   Teacher's Strategy Toolbox: Designed with   101
the Student and Teacher in Mind

Ten   Teacher Traits: What Makes a Great Teacher?   126

References   133

Index   135

Preface

This book began, after a conversation with my Heinemann editor, Lois Bridges, as a work on classroom management. Although I tried to focus on the classroom management techniques that had made my students so successful and my classroom years increasingly effective, I couldn't isolate management techniques from my total approach to teaching and learning. After several false starts, Lois and I agreed that when teaching strategies are based on how we learn, when the teacher focuses on student outcomes, and, most especially, when students are given the responsibility and the tools to manage and monitor their own learning, then effective classroom management is a by-product.

This book is about classroom management, but it's about classroom management in its broadest sense; classroom management that is invisible. What you will find in these pages is a classroom structure in which all students can learn, where students take charge of their own learning and behavior and are thus more motivated and better able to learn. This is a classroom where the teacher is more effective but actually works a lot less.

The single most important ingredient in student success, especially for many of our students who come from academically disadvantaged settings, is the quality of the teacher. Good teachers establish and maintain the classroom environment, introduce the instructional and behavioral goals and why they are important, and work together with students, their families, and community members toward meeting those goals.

When all constituents—teacher, parents, and students—contribute, and all have ownership and responsibility and are held accountable, then there is order. You won't need an elaborate system to monitor behavior because it's the disenfranchised student who is most likely to act out, and the engaged students who monitor their own behavior.

The classroom structure and the teaching strategies presented in the following pages, when used together, create an academic setting where all students are successful, where truly No Child Is Left Behind.

Adrienne Mack-Kirschner, Ed.D.
National Board Certified Teacher

Acknowledgments

This book didn't happen overnight, nor did I create the classroom management system described in these pages out of thin air. So many educators and others contributed to my development as a classroom teacher, mentor, professional development consultant, and writer that it would be impossible to thank them each by name. So I'll begin with a great big heartfelt thank-you to all the teachers I've ever had, and to the wonderful teachers in my family: my sister Royce Bellatty and brother-in-law Bill; cousin Susie Pavane; daughters Christine Simon and Roxanne Ross; and son-in-law David Ross. I've watched you, learned from you, and maybe even contributed to your progress as well. My mentee Lisa Jones pushed my buttons and conducted student-led conferences with me when no one else in our school wanted any part of them. When I told Lisa I was thinking of writing a book on classroom management, she laughed because she knew that our classroom management was always about relevant teaching. English teachers Ron Harris and Dave Muskrath forced me, through their inquiry and desire to know more and do more for their students, to continue my own learning. I've benefited from numerous educators, especially from principal Greg Vallone, who never doubted that I could help him to move his school forward. I want to thank Percy Clark, superintendent of the Pasadena Unified School District, who, through his honest struggles to make PUSD the best possible learning environment for students, pushed me to investigate and question and admit that this is hard work worth doing well.

A big thank-you goes to my husband, keeper of the coffee pot, who keeps me grounded, and the coffee beans ground; to Michael Bass, vice president of Hy-Ko Products, for helping me to keep learning real; to Lois Bridges, my editor at Heinemann, who is always open to my ideas and is not shy about challenging them when they need to be challenged; and to Oklahoma teacher and friend Jeanne Owens, who was the first to read this manuscript and who reminded me to pause for reflection.

How to Use This Book:
A Friendly Instruction Manual

Do not confine your children to your own learning, for they were born in another time.

■Hebrew Proverb

Straight Talk for Today's Teacher presents a philosophy for teaching and learning that moves the emphasis from what the teacher does to what the student learns. This book contains strategies, and explains why they work so well to create and maintain a learning environment where rewards come from demonstrating accomplishment, not from accumulating points. The hundreds of teachers who have participated in my workshops during the last dozen years have successfully used these methods to increase student learning while reducing their own workload. For many of you, these strategies will be new. For others, they will be an expansion of what you are already doing, or used to do, or have thoughts about doing. In order to make the more abstract philosophical concepts more concrete, I've isolated the driving themes that distinguish this way of being and teaching from more traditional, teacher-centered approaches. But if you prefer, go straight to the strategies and return for theory at a future time.

When I condense my thoughts until I can squeeze them no further I am left with a single word, *mindfulness*. To teach well is to be mindful of all that you do, all that you ask of students, and all that you receive from them. This book is about mindful teaching.

To receive the greatest benefit from the practices and ideas in this book you should first spend time analyzing their philosophical base. I recommend that your first reading be a quick one; allow the overall philosophy to resonate within you before implementing the strategies. Discuss the ideas with your colleagues. Imagine how your teaching might be different if you adopted one or more of the recommended strategies, beginning with the end in mind. For example, *what would it be like for you, for your students, and for their families, if you held student-led conferences throughout the year? What if you facilitated strategies that were heavily dependent on students talking with and teaching one another?*

If students selected the topics for their research and projects, would you be able to trust them to make valuable decisions?

Mindful teaching depends on turning the learning over to students and learning along with them. Unfortunately, in most classrooms where I have had the opportunity to observe, teachers are doing more of the work and students are doing—and learning—less. It should be the other way around—teachers doing less so students do more and learn more.

Take some time to reflect on each of the following questions and statements that define the philosophy underlying the strategies in this book. This is time well spent and may make the difference between a successful implementation and a less effective one.

1. Consider in advance everything you do in the classroom and everything you ask students to do.

2. Learning and retention are highest when students are actively engaged. What are you currently doing that students can and should be doing?

3. Information is available to anyone who seeks it; redefine your role from keeper and disseminator of information to guide and facilitator.

4. Identify the skills necessary for success in the twenty-first century, learn them yourself, then teach them to students.

5. Open your doors and let your colleagues in—as collaborators, as observers, as critics.

6. Invite and expect families to be actively involved in their children's education.

7. Allow time for rest, reflection, and rejuvenation—for yourself and for your students.

8. A healthy exchange of ideas can only occur in an emotionally safe environment.

9. Change in itself is neither a benefit nor a detriment. Continue instructional practices that foster student engagement and learning and discontinue those that don't.

10. Student work improves when the audience extends beyond the teacher.

11. Learning to ask open-ended questions is as important as answering them, maybe more so.

12. When teaching focuses on learning, revision is encouraged and redemption is applauded. What might revision and redemption look like in your teaching practice?

13. Thinking takes time and cannot be easily measured. But action without thinking can take even more time and be ultimately less productive. We don't learn from our experiences; we do learn by thinking about our experiences.

We sometimes rush to take action, to implement a strategy, even before we think through our long- and short-term goals. Teachers who come to personally own the philosophy underlying the strategies in this book are more likely to be able to adapt them to form a perfect fit with their own practice. Nothing contained here has to be adopted as is. Feel free to mold the strategies to fit your teaching style and learning as well as the students' learning. Pause frequently along the way to reflect on your own teaching and learning. I've included reflections at the end of some chapters. Make decisions and changes based on the students' learning because *it is all about them*.

Straight Talk for Today's Teacher

Chapter One

Teaching with the Brain in Mind

The Brain Has a Mind of Its Own

The human brain is an amazing structure—a universe of infinite possibilities and mystery. It constantly shapes and reshapes itself as a result of experience, yet it can take off on its own without input from the outside world. How does it form a human mind, capture experience, or stop time in memory? Although it does not generate enough energy to light a simple bulb, its capabilities make it the most powerful force on earth.

■David A. Sousa, *How the Brain Learns*

"The good news is that the more we discover about how the brain learns, the more successful teaching and learning can be. The bad news is that we cannot get this information to teachers fast enough" (Sousa 1995, xiv). This chapter provides an overview of how we learn. It is not a comprehensive guide but rather an attempt to get information about the brain to teachers in a timely and efficient manner. It is included so we can discuss throughout the book why some strategies work and others don't—in spite of teachers' and students' best efforts. Most of the information contained here has been condensed from the works of Drs. David Sousa (1995) and Rita Smilkstein (2003). Both are excellent resources for additional study and for pictures and diagrams about how the brain looks. We focus here on the brain and learning.

Input

• We are born to learn; we begin thinking even before birth.
  Learning is pleasant when it is active, relevant, and meaningful.

"Young children 'think, observe, and reason. They consider evidence, draw conclusions, do experiments, solve problems, and search for the truth'" (Smilkstein 2003, 26). My twenty-two-month old grandson, Jake, has had a remote control in his hand since he found one on the sofa. He can load the VHS, set the channel, and play a video forward and backward—tasks I continue to struggle with. Jake's parents, both teachers, sometimes step aside so Jake can learn through trial and error, at his own pace, and in his own way.

- The more you use your brain, the greater its capacity. You can't use it up, or fill it up, or know so much there's no room for anything else.

- The richer the learning experience, the higher the motivation, the greater the learning. This is a good argument for not "dumbing down" the student work or your expectations for your students. They may need more scaffolding if they don't have a solid background, but they can learn. You can placate students with worksheets and word searches, but you can't motivate them to push themselves toward higher levels of achievement if you only provide low, domesticating work they don't consider relevant or important.

- The number of brain cells is finite; you have what you have. But with use, the brain improves. Cells increase in size; the branches connecting cells get stronger; the nerve networks become more complex. All of which aids retention and learning.

- Sight, hearing, and touch contribute to about 95 percent of all new learning over the course of our lifetime. Be cautious about how much importance you attach to the multiple intelligence classifications described by Howard Gardner. Although we may have strengths in one or more areas, most of our learning comes through sight, hearing, and touch.

- "I think, therefore I'm thin." Learning is good for the figure because the brain, although it only represents about 3 percent of your weight, burns about 20 percent of the calories you take in. The more complex the learning, the more fuel you burn. Therefore, the more thinking, the thinner you're likely to be. Because the brain demands high-quality caloric intake to operate efficiently, it is especially important that students come to school well fed. You can't learn well on an empty stomach. Keeping a supply of emergency energy bars in your desk drawer may pay dividends on test day. Reconsider any rules you may have about no drinking in class; a dehydrated brain is inefficient.

- High-priority data overrides low-priority data. What a student perceives as most important to learn or to input is what takes precedence. Therefore, if the student is concentrating on getting the attention of the girl across the room, or being safe and not looking like a fool in front of his classmates, he most likely won't learn anything else. If the student needs to use the bathroom, or thirsts for a drink of water, or feels too hot, that data also prevails over learning. We learn best in an emotionally safe, physically comfortable environment. Consider how your classroom environment affects learning.
- Adolescents generally can handle about fifteen to twenty minutes of concentration before needing a break, drifting away, or getting bored—and that's on a very good day with interesting, relevant curriculum! Consider chunking lessons by changing the activity every fifteen or twenty minutes—lectures definitely cannot exceed twenty minutes or most, maybe all, will be lost.

Relevance

- To learn it, we first have to understand it; we have to make a connection to prior knowledge, and we have to want to learn it. If it's not perceived as relevant for us, we don't learn it. When you take the time to help students to make the connections, learning happens. Begin instruction by stating why this information or skill is meaningful and important beyond the moment. Hook into what is important for your students' lives, presently and in the future. Connect to what they already know.

What Stays

- The more we connect what we are learning to what we already know, the greater the understanding and retention.
- The short-term memory holds data only for about thirty seconds. Truly in one ear and out the other. That's why we have to practice, practice, and then practice.
- Working memory can only handle a few bits of information at a time. Sorting information into meaningful chunks is a good thing so each bit is bigger. We can handle about five to nine bits of data.
- We store information in long-term memory, bit by bit, new on top of old. The combinations are endless. Hence, no two of us have the same

collection of memories. We may think we are providing the same input, but each student records new information according to what is already there, what is considered meaningful and relevant at the time, and the degree of emotional safety and comfort in place. No two students learn exactly the same thing at the same time in the same way.

The Smart Get Smarter

- The brain actively constructs its own knowledge. We add new information based on what we already know. The first information forms the foundation for all subsequent learning; we try to make the new information fit onto the old information. Thus, it is critically important that we know what the students already know, especially if they hold prior misconceptions. Misconceptions should be addressed directly and explicitly or the new learning may be negatively impacted. Everything we teach must be connected to something the students already know; you can't do that if you don't know what they know. To find out, ask them.

- Not all students will learn new material at the same rate. The learning rate is dependent, partially, on what the student already knows. Students who are labeled as slow learners are often learners who lack background information. Thus, it is very important to know what students already know, or don't know.

- Readers get smarter; nonreaders get dumber relative to their peer group and grade level. Because everything we read, fiction and nonfiction, is about something, readers are continually building background knowledge. Thus they have more "learning Velcro" in place on which to stick the new learning. Those who don't read widely don't have extensive background information on which to build new learning. Reading is more than just about reading, it's about growing a knowledge base. We read to learn and to enable ourselves to learn.

- Students will readily participate in learning activities that have yielded success for them in the past and avoid those that have produced failure.

Output Impacts Retention

- Retention improves dramatically when we transform what we learn into creative products. We take the learning and make it ours.

That's why doing projects, ones we really think about and work on over time, help us reinforce and extend our learning. A creative product can be a drawing, a musical composition, an essay, a speech, or any number of projects that engage our interest—even a lesson we teach to others. Provide multiple paths for completion. Output should be about high quality not just about quantity.

- Rehearsal is essential. If students don't apply it, they won't remember it. They need to assign the learning value and relevance, or it's gone. More time spent on task, not more new material, improves long-term retention. Going deeper, not broader, improves learning. It's crucial to determine what learning goals are most important and teach to those and not try to cover every bit of material.

- Every time we retrieve information from our memory, it's like learning it again; we reinforce the memory. If we only call on the first hands that go up, the rest of the class shuts off the retrieval process and misses an opportunity to reinforce more learning. Instead, ask all students to think about the question for at least thirty seconds. Don't allow any hands to be raised until you see students are engaged in the question.

- The average time teachers wait before responding to their own questions or asking another student the same question is about three seconds! Teach yourself to wait. After lots of practice I can wait up to three minutes before moving on. Allow the students to struggle, allow time for retrieval, allow for those students who need more retrieval time, to have it. Don't equate first hand up with smarter—there's not always a direct connection. Likewise, don't assume hands that don't go up mean the students don't know. They may just need more time for retrieval.

- Consider stopping the lesson before the bell rings and allow students to gather their thoughts. Have students keep learning journals. What did I learn today? Help students to get in the habit of thinking about their learning.

Knowing How to Teach so Students Learn

- Best learning occurs at the beginning of the period, second best at the end. Therefore, don't have students start the class with incorrect information. That's what is likely to be learned.

Teaching with
the Brain in Mind

- Think about how your teaching strategies affect student learning. Dr. David Sousa provides this learning pyramid for retention of information after twenty-four hours:

  - lecture   5 percent retention
  - reading   10 percent
  - audiovisual   20 percent
  - demonstration   30 percent
  - discussion group   50 percent
  - practice by doing   75 percent
  - immediate use of learning (teaching others)   90 percent

- Teaching less and letting students do more is real teaching. School should not be about the teacher doing everything. Teachers working harder are not better for students. Students working more and working smarter add to greater and more permanent learning. Student Effort + Effective Strategies = Success

- Strategies that encourage students to construct knowledge, which is then enhanced or reinforced by teachers, boosts student learning. Lectures, vocabulary, explanations, and so on should come *after* students have spent some time trying to understand.

- The Zone of Proximal Development (Vygotsky 1896–1934): Vygotsky's work identified a zone to target for learning. This zone is somewhat above what students already know, enough to challenge them. But not so far above what they already know or are able to do that they are frustrated and give up. Although you might set high instructional goals, students will reach only as far as they believe they can be successful. Break the task down into consumable parts and scaffold learning. Remember, you can't do this if you don't know what the students already know.

- Bringing the world into the classroom, creating global awareness, taking students out into the world, virtually or in reality, and allowing for student *inter*action and *intra*action increases learning and retention.

- Teachers don't have to know it all. Allow students to become the experts and teach others, including you. If you are technologically challenged, like me, you can begin by letting them run the classroom technology, at which they are usually quite skilled.

- Helping students find connections between their learning objectives and their current and future worlds is essential for motivation and improves attitudes about learning. Engagement leads to higher academic achievement, lower dropout rates, better attendance, and better college preparation. And it makes teaching easier and more pleasant.

- To learn at high levels, we have to first know the basics. Assess students for basic knowledge and literal understanding before moving on to application and critical thinking. We can't manipulate ideas until we are grounded in the basic information and skills on which these ideas depend.

- Teachers need to front-load, to spend more time in the beginning laying the foundation. KWL (Know, Want to know, Learn) is an excellent strategy and should be in every teacher's repertoire. I devote a whole chapter to this strategy and several variations because it has so many applications and works so well—it's brain compatible. Because we can't make the leap or grow out of a void, we have to begin with what the students know and go from there.

- Begin with the end in mind—the goals or objectives, deconstruct them, determine what skills, what bits of knowledge are necessary to get to the goals, then build one skill on top of another.

Every educator should know something about how the brain learns. When our teaching strategies, or the curriculum or mandated pacing plan, go counter to how the brain learns, learning doesn't happen. Use this information about the brain to inform your teaching. Let the students in on this information; I've never met a student who wasn't fascinated by learning about their own learning. Knowing how the brain builds knowledge sets the stage for establishing class norms that focus on learning.

Use the quiz in Figure 1–1 for a class discussion on how we learn. (Hint: all the answers are TRUE.)

Student Quiz: The Brain and Learning

Instructions: Answer true or false to each of the statements below. Be prepared to back up your response with an example from your own learning.

No.	Statement	True	False
1.	Children's brains work exactly the same way adult brains work.		
2.	You can learn anything given sufficient time and effort.		
3.	We can unlearn things that we want to unlearn, like bad habits.		
4.	The smart get smarter. The more we read and study, the more we know; the more we learn, the more we can learn.		
5.	We learn best what we practice.		
6.	Readers get smarter; nonreaders get dumber, and dumber, and dumber.		
7.	The brain is an organ that gets stronger and more efficient with more practice.		
8.	Our brains need proper nutrition. We need nutrients, the right chemicals, including potassium. Eat bananas. (Maybe that's why apes are smart.)		
9.	Emotions are activated more frequently in an adolescent brain than in an adult brain.		
10.	Students who feel happy and safe learn better.		
11.	Making mistakes and then correcting them improves learning and retention.		
12.	Due to our DNA we may have an aptitude to learn one thing more quickly than another.		
13.	Given time, effort, and strong modeling we can learn whatever we set out to learn.		

FIGURE 1–1 Student Quiz: The Brain and Learning

Chapter Two

Classroom Environment
It All Begins with You

A learning space must be hospitable—inviting as well as open, safe and trustworthy, as well as free . . . [It] must have features that help students deal with the dangers of an educational expedition: places to rest, places to find nourishment, even places to seek shelter when one feels overexposed.

■Parker Palmer, *The Courage to Teach*

Establishing a classroom environment that supports learning like the one Parker Palmer describes takes time initially, but saves time over the course of the year. Whether we're establishing an inviting classroom environment, getting to know the students in our classes, reading good literature, or examining the big ideas in science or social studies, we need to spend our time and resources on what we value most. Consider devoting time during the first week of school to building classroom community and to establishing specific short- and long-term course goals. Once established, your community of learners will pick up speed and amaze you with how much and how well they master the curriculum.

A Good Reputation

Building a learning community begins before students even approach your classroom door. It begins with your reputation, what former students say about you and how they say it. If you love teaching, if it's your passion, if you love children, especially the teenagers who walk into your room, and you respect the community where they live, you're well on your way to establishing a learning community where students will take risks and learn and struggle and try again. Likewise, if your school reputation is unfavorable, if students enter the classroom in fight mode, their negative attitude will deflect from their learning. If you have to make some repairs, do so.

Chaos

A classroom environment that supports learning requires very strong classroom management, but in the most effective, student-centered classrooms the management part is nearly invisible. I concur with Robert Marzano's findings that "of all the variables, classroom management has the largest effect on student achievement. This makes intuitive sense—students cannot learn in a chaotic, poorly managed classroom" (Marzano 2003, 88). Although students know you are the final authority, they should feel that the classroom belongs to them, as does the responsibility for their learning. The most effective classrooms are those in which the students manage and monitor their own behavior to support learning.

Meeting and Greeting

It is important, especially during the first week of school, to greet your students at the door, invite them in, and encourage them to get comfortable by finding a place where they like to sit. Learn their names as quickly as possible. I observe too many classrooms in our large secondary schools where, even at the end of the semester, teachers don't know all the students by name and classmates don't know one another's names. How can we expect students to work in cooperative settings or engage in meaningful discussions if students are pointing to one another, saying, "He said," or referring to another student as "The girl in the blue sweater" because the name is not known?

Although I have great difficulty with names, even the names of adults I see frequently, I struggle to learn every child's name by the end of the first week. I was reminded recently of how dehumanizing it is not to be called by name. On an auto trip to northern California I passed the driving time listening to tunes from the musical *Les Misérables*. In one of the many poignant songs, Inspector Gilbert repeatedly refers to Jean Valjean as 62038. Each time I heard the number I winced. Using the prisoner's number, not his name, strips away the person's identity and reduces the freed Valjean to prisoner status again. Although this example may be extreme, not calling our students by name, or not even knowing their names, has a similar, chilling effect. When you don't know a student's name, the student feels invisible.

As the school year progresses make a point to learn something about each student. Incorporate your knowledge into your greetings. *Hi,*

Juan, how is your mother feeling? Maria, did the dance go well Saturday night? George, over the weekend I saw a model ship similar to the one you showed me you were building; it was really cool. Samantha, the description in your essay about chocolate sauce tempted me to break my diet. Or a more general greeting, like *Hey Bobbi, how's the day treating you?* Nearly any well-intended remark that you direct to a student will have a positive effect. "Showing students that you value their interests, cultures, and life experiences helps foster healthy relationships" (Wolk 1998, 14).

The Name Game

After the students find a place to sit on the first day, I ask them to make sure they are in a seat that fits them well because they will not be able to change seats during the first week. That's the time we'll need to get to know one another by name. Following my announcement, there's generally some seat shuffling, which is fine, and then they settle in. With a seating chart in hand, I ask each student to clearly state her name and any nick-name she might prefer we use in class. I repeat each name as I write it, in pencil, on the seating chart. I go to the second person and follow the same procedure except that after I write and state the second name, I repeat the first. When I write the third name, I repeat the first and second names. Then I ask the students to pay attention because we're going to see who can state the name of every person in the class. It becomes a game, not a competition, because there's no points awarded or prizes meted out. The reward is getting to know one another, and being known. Everyone can accomplish the task. I begin every class that first week with a recall of everyone's name, depending less and less on the seating chart as the week progresses. Learning everyone's name, especially when your total class load may exceed 150 students per day, takes time and commitment, but it's well worth your efforts, and your students'. Insist that students call you, and one another, by name. They will respond well knowing that you care enough to take the time to know who they are.

Clean and Green Rooms

In our urban school district most of the school buildings are old, painted either gunmetal gray or drab beige. They have windows that don't open; those that do are often covered with iron grating. Nevertheless, it is amazing how warm the environment becomes when

I add some live green plants, a lava lamp purchased at a garage sale, and a donated sofa. No classroom is complete without a radio or CD player and a stack of collected CDs. I save the wall space for student work interspersed with inspirational slogans. We commit to keeping the room clean. It's not unusual for me to begin the class, or end it, with a quick cleanup. If the floor needs sweeping, I hand a student a broom with instructions to sweep a section then hand the broom off. Occasionally there's some rumbling, but the students appreciate that the room looks nice for them. Keeping the room clean comes with allowing more flexibility about eating and drinking in class. Privileges carry responsibility—a message my students hear often.

Ask students and their families to contribute plants for the classrooms, brooms and cleaning supplies, a goldfish bowl, or an old sofa. Collect quarters, if necessary, to purchase a boom box (too big to hide in a backpack). The more students and their families are involved in putting the room together, the more they will be respectful of what is there.

Sounds and Smells

Just as the sight of the room is important, so are the sounds and the smells. Putting forty hormone-producing teens in a hot classroom every hour makes the room pretty ripe. Keep lightly scented candles or air fresheners around. Be sensitive to students' allergies by using a non-allergy-producing scent. Music soothes the savage beast. There have been numerous studies done on how students react to music. A Mozart concerto played during middle school lunch periods is known to have a calming effect on students and results in fewer fights. Music playing in the background acts like a white noise to mask other unwanted noises.

Books, Books, and Then More Books

Surround your classroom with print materials: books, magazines, student publications, local newspapers, poetry collections, graphic novels (comic books), student work, advertisements, and anything the students bring in. My friend and colleague Alfee Enciso uses inexpensive plastic rain gutters to create book shelves on his bulletin boards. The rain gutters supplement traditional book shelves and work especially well for displaying books, magazines, and other print materials with their full covers showing. There's something more enticing about choosing a book when you can see more than the spine.

Maintain a wide collection of fiction and nonfiction at multiple reading levels. I always have a wide assortment of picture books, especially the favorites like *Flat Stanley* and several versions of the classics like *Cinderella* and *Cinder Ella*, and *The Real Story of the 3 Little Pigs*. You may find, as I do, that struggling students need a way to jump into reading, and picture books, read in a safe environment where no one will embarrass them, may be just what they need.

Maintain a binder with your writing, including anything you've published, to share with students. This can be an effective model of learning for students.

Beliefs and Biases

We teach based on what we believe about our students. If we think they can't learn, we won't expect much. If we think they are dishonest, we'll lock away our possessions and the class resources and confine them to their seats. When we believe they can learn, we set high expectations. Ask yourself what you believe about your students.

Try this exercise: Without stopping to censor your ideas, list at least ten words or phrases that come to mind when you think about your students. When the list is complete reread it, considering the implications for teaching and learning behind each of the characteristics you've listed. If your list has words or phrases like *disrespectful, pushy, dumb*, or *lazy*, ask yourself how your beliefs might contribute to students' behaviors. What do you need to do to change their performance?

The words I've listed above are pretty extreme, deliberately so. When I've done this exercise with teachers they frequently try to steer clear of any negative words, even if they have felt them rise to the surface. Be honest. It's only by confronting our own beliefs that we can create the best learning environment possible. We first have to respect our students, our colleagues, and ourselves.

My list changes from time to time. How I feel about my students depends on what's been happening at school and at home, the reading I'm doing for work or leisure, and the experiences I'm having in and out of the classroom. The list becomes more negative when I don't take the time for rest and rejuvenation. Too much work, too many papers to grade, mandates to follow, and students to discipline make me grumpy and negative. Find time for rejuvenation—your students deserve it.

Classroom Environment

Because I now work primarily with teachers, they are my students. Here's my latest unedited list: Teachers are caring; struggling; stressed and overworked; lazy and hiding out in their classrooms; in the wrong profession; dedicated. They need more strategies and more content knowledge—much higher-quality professional development; need more time to think; want to make a difference; have mixed ability levels; want to help all kids.

In rereading the list, different from the one I did last week or from one I'll do in a week or two, I know that I have to be careful about expecting less from the teachers. I also know that my work with them, as coach, mentor, or professional development specialist can't add to their stress. Every time I do this exercise I examine how my beliefs affect the work I do with teachers.

Loving Your Subject

This year I'm working with a new group of National Board Certification candidates. During introductions, one teacher stated how much she dislikes her new assignment; she doesn't believe the integrated science approach will yield any good results. If you find yourself in this position, hating the subject(s) or grade level, either change your assignment or find something in it that you can love. If you don't value the course, as this teacher expressed, your students won't value it either. They will also feel like they are a burden, they've gotten between what you have to teach and what you want to teach. Good teaching begins with knowledge and passion about what we're teaching and who we are teaching to. Love it or leave it!

Organization

In order to provide a safe and comfortable environment for myself and for my students, I organize the room to support learning. Within the constraints of the room itself, I position supplies and resources where everyone will have the most convenient access.

Everything has a place. Staplers are available for anyone to use at any time, but when finished they belong on the edge of my desk. Dictionaries, likewise available for anytime reference, go on the top shelf in the bookshelf to the rear of the room. The boom box is close to me (I want ultimate control of volume and music played). The TV/VCR, when we have one, is in a far corner where it's less of a distraction and so students won't be asking, "Are we going to see a film today?" My desk is generally off to the front side of the room, which gives me a good view, affords some privacy, and sends the message that I'm not the center of the universe, or the classroom.

Routines

Routines are comfortable. We know we'll be following the routines most of the time and won't have to think about them too much so we can focus on the learning.

Agendas

Agendas provide a guide map for students and me. They list the activities for the day and note upcoming due dates. Posting the agenda on the board has become a critical element. Students enter the room and immediately copy the agenda into their notebooks. It's the only rote copying I require; there are good reasons. The agenda is a skeletal outline of what we're doing in class and what and when assignments are due. I post an agenda for each class, labeling them period 1, or 2, or 5 and 6, depending on what courses I'm teaching that semester. I never label the agendas "Honors English," "Regular English," "Remedial." Students know which classes they are in, they don't need to be reminded if they are in a lower-level English class. As much as possible the agendas look the same.

Here's how agendas make your work easier:

1. Students know what is happening that day.

2. Students are alerted to assignment due dates, even those that may be weeks away.

3. Absent students can copy the agenda from any student in attendance without having to ask, "What did we do while I was absent?"

4. Absent students are responsible for makeup work; they don't ask me, they ask another student.

5. If we'll need portfolios, textbooks, or other resources, I post that on the agenda as well. In this way students know what they will need for class that day and can get their supplies before sitting down.

6. Posting the due dates removes the excuse that they didn't know when the work was due. With few exceptions, I don't accept late

Classroom Environment

work when the student could turn it in early, or give it to someone else to turn in if they will be absent.

7. With five or more classes to teach each day, by mid-morning I sometimes forget what I planned. The agenda reminds me without my having to return to the lesson-planning book.

Take a look at Figure 2–1 to see a typical agenda.

FIGURE 2–1
Typical Agenda

Periods 1 and 3 American Lit.	Periods 2 and 6 Expository Comp.	Period 4 Journalism
Portfolio and textbook	Check draft—persuasive essay	Assignments to editors NOW
Collect homework	Read-arounds	Report on ads sold
Read Ben Franklin	Discussion	Editor in Chief meeting
Discussion	Revision	Paper to printer—Thursday
Journal writing	Essays due on Friday	
Book reports due March 12		
Field trip permission slips due now	Senior prom tickets on sale in students' store	Next assignment meeting on Monday—Think about what you want to write

Agendas are not carved in stone and are likely to change somewhat during the course of the day. I stay alert to teachable moments, altering plans to fit the learning. Sometimes we need more time than I originally planned and we carry over an activity to the next day, or we abandon one that didn't work. Agendas are guides that help us to focus and to be more productive—thus allowing time for other activities we may want to add during the course of the semester.

I learned early on that if I wanted students to copy agendas I had to hold them accountable in some way. I added the agendas to student portfolios (see Chapter Six).

The Learning Journal

Most days close with a learning journal entry. What did I learn today? What surprised me? What do I have questions about? What do I want to know more about? As a closing activity the learning journal works well. Students pay more attention during class knowing they will have to make an entry about their day's learning. Questions still unanswered aren't forgotten. We begin the next class by reviewing the learning journal entries, starting with unanswered questions. It's one of the simplest strategies I use on a regular basis, and one of the most effective.

I don't read all entries, although I do collect them periodically because what isn't collected doesn't get done—unfortunately. For each journal I flip through the pages and write one comment in response. Something easy: "I had the same question" or "I'm glad you got this, I also found it interesting." You can generally determine the student's engagement by reading one or two entries. Those who take it more seriously really try to capture the day's learning, they ask questions that are thoughtful.

As with all other routines, I wish I could report that every student in every class is learning at their highest possible level, but that would not be true. Students seldom slip through but some do decide not to accomplish the goals. It is most rare to have a student, by semester's end, blame anyone but themselves for not being successful, especially since there are ample opportunities for revision, reconstruction, and redemption.

Raising Your Hand

No rule in place about this. The activity determines whether or not hand raising is appropriate. If the class is working individually and I'm roaming about the room, raising your hand gets my attention and doesn't interrupt anyone else. In a class discussion, students generally raise their hands, but might also jump in. When determining which rules you need to operate efficiently, be mindful. What's the purpose? What's the likely effect on student behavior? Do the positives outweigh any negative? Then decide. Don't be concerned about changing your mind during the year, or having slightly different routines for each class. Each class has its own personality and may exhibit different behaviors. Be flexible and thoughtful.

Kids out of Control

As a coach, I'm sometimes called upon by a teacher, or his principal, to assist with classroom management. We may begin the coaching session with a complaint, "This class is out of control. I can't do anything with them." I'll then ask the teacher, using the roll book, to identify each student who is out of control. Usually, the list is quite short, seldom more than three students. We then identify some positive traits of the offending students. That's where we focus our attention. How do we increase these traits and associated behaviors and decrease the offending ones? I'm not a Pollyanna thinking that if we believe something positive about a student that child will be transformed, but it's a beginning. Find something good to say, and then say it often, say it so others can hear, say it so the student can hear. Positive feedback is just as effective in changing behaviors as it is in moving a student forward in their academic learning.

The Classroom Monitor

One of the most effective strategies I've ever used with a kid who was out of control is to turn control over to him. This technique works best in middle school where the kids still relish tattling on someone else. I take the worst offender, the most disruptive student, and make him or her Sheriff for the day. The student Sheriff sits in one corner of the room, preferably on a high stool. The Sheriff has a clipboard and a thick yellow pad (which he doesn't really need, but which makes him feel more important). The instructions are to record every student's behavior every five minutes. The Sheriff visually sweeps the room writing down what each student is doing—paying attention, getting out of the seat, talking to a neighbor, working in the group, sleeping, reading silently, reading out loud, etc. During the last five minutes of the period the Sheriff reads from his list telling what each student did in each five-minute interval. Mostly, the Sheriff attends to those students whom he believes aren't doing what they should be doing—behaviors he can spot because he knows them so well. At the end of the period, after the others have left, the Sheriff and I talk about the impact of student misbehavior, and the impact of his past misbehavior. This is not, unfortunately, a permanent cure for the chronically disruptive. But it helps, and at the very least removes the offending student for the day without banishing him to the office. The unexpected result is that everyone wants a turn to be Sheriff, which I usually grant once a week until our collective interest runs out.

Inviting All Students to Learn

Several years ago I conducted a student focus group at an urban high school. The participants were hand selected by the dean; he knew them all on a first-name basis. What they told me after we established trust was chilling. They spoke of teachers who asked them why they bothered to come to school at all; who told them they can't learn so get a job; and who made lots of other humiliating remarks. Had I not also heard these comments from teachers griping about poor student attendance and participation, I may have discounted the students' words. But I knew they were true. I asked the students how hearing this made them feel.

At-risk kids have feelings too. You may only hear their attitudes, see their sauntering and *I don't really care* swagger, and record a series of absences, but these are still children who didn't wake up that morning plotting, *what can I do today to help myself fail?* The fact that they are walking into your classroom at all, especially after a long absence, or without the completed homework, or not having the textbooks they know they should be carrying, speaks more about how much they want to learn, than about what they didn't do. They just don't know how to get into the school groove, but you can help.

Try greeting the returning student with, *Hey, it's great to see you. Glad you're here.* Or, *You're going to love what we're reading, or studying, or doing, take a seat.* Almost anything you say that is not negative, that doesn't have a barbed sarcastic comment attached, lets the student and the rest of the class know that you care about each of them. Every day counts.

The Incorrigible

Although I consider it a personal failure when I don't reach a student, those students do exist. Sometimes it's a bad mix—you and that student just don't belong in the same space. More often, though, the student has issues you can't resolve in your classroom. You must be an advocate for all of your students and remove the student who consistently disrupts everyone else's learning. Do whatever it takes until you have resolution. We can do the very best we can, try lots of strategies, but sometimes we are not able to solve all of the problems students bring to class that get in the way of learning. Don't try to go it alone. Enlist the principal, the parents, your colleagues, and when all else fails, the union rep. Most of our students are in school to learn; it is unconscionable to allow a single student's disruptive behavior to prevent others from achieving.

Even the Gifted

I read that of every ten high school dropouts, two are gifted. These are the kids who stare at the floor in boredom, who may not do their assignments—not because they can't, but because they are demeaning and boring, asking too little of them. Many of our gifted students are not identified as gifted; therefore every classroom needs a range of resource materials, unabridged dictionaries, a variety of books and professional magazines that are way beyond the students' tested reading levels. Projects and other assignments need to be open-ended to allow students to stretch themselves. I wish I had studied giftedness (I'm doing this now), even though I always taught regular classes and had a special affinity for at-risk students. I would have been a more effective teacher by offering more high-level opportunities in my regular program. Educate yourself on markers identifying gifted students. These include a high level of intensity, comfort with complexity, seriousness, rapid learning ability, personal sensitivity and compassion, perfectionism, unusual curiosity, and a high degree of energy. Don't just teach to the middle; provide opportunities to stretch everyone.

Questioning Rules

Think about every rule you've ever seen posted in a classroom. A rule mandating that students raise their hands before speaking might dispel commotion, but it also puts an end to quality discussions, an important strategy to promote literacy and critical thinking. *No getting out of your seat without the teacher's permission* appears to be reasonable, until the students don't use dictionaries or other reference materials they might benefit from. And *no drinking water?* If you're tired, or hungry, or thirsty, you can't focus on learning. And if you have to use the bathroom, but the rules are that you have to wait until the bell rings, you're definitely not going to be able to concentrate on your studies. School and classroom rules should all support learning; do yours?

Silence Is Not Golden

If you want to minimize how often rules are broken, follow a students' biology in determining what rules are worth enforcing. For teens it's natural to be moving and talking; it's unnatural to sit without moving for twenty minutes or more. Humans are innately social. Therefore, when we set up environments that do not honor social exchanges, there are going to be problems. Room layout is critical and should be fluid, whenever possible, to support the learning activity. Rows are great for listening to lectures, grouped seating works well for projects, Socratic circles for whole-class discussions. When I went to high school in New York the desks were bolted to the floor. A rare few wise educators ripped out the bolts and provided moveable desks—use them whenever possible.

One of the goals of public schooling is to prepare our graduates to be active participants in a democratic society. But we don't prepare students for democracy when we don't model democracy in the classroom. Give them some freedom, allow them a voice, and set the stage for ownership in their own learning. Classrooms that silence children impede learning.

Learning Communities

Every student who walks into your classroom is already a learner. They've learned to walk, talk, and dress themselves. Most have learned to read and write and think about issues that are important to them, some better than others. They've learned to ride bicycles, roller blade, and skate board. What they may not have done, however, is paid attention to how they learned. Helping your students identify how they learn sets the stage for establishing class norms, a student-friendly alternative to teacher-set rules. Prepare to model for them based on your own good and bad learning experiences. Here's mine:

I learn best when: (1) I'm studying something I want to know; (2) I know something about the topic already so the new information or skill doesn't make me feel stupid; (3) I have enough time; (4) I believe the learning will help me to achieve a goal I've set for myself; and (5) the learning target is interesting, exciting, strange, funny, or otherwise grabs my attention.

I don't learn well when: (1) the target is so far above me that I don't believe I'll ever get it; (2) I feel rushed; (3) it's someone else's agenda and not what I want to do or know; (4) it's so noisy I can't concentrate; and (5) I disagree but am not allowed to voice my opinion.

What conditions help you to learn and what hinder your learning? Knowing those factors that set the stage for your learning and those factors that inhibit your learning will help you select teaching strategies and create a classroom environment that supports learning for you and for your students. When you ask your students to identify the conditions that support or impede their learning, prepare to share yours. Don't confuse the conditions supporting learning with learning style (visual, auditory, bodily-kinesthetic, linguistic, logical-mathematical, spatial, musical, interpersonal, intrapersonal), as identified in Howard Gardner's Multiple Intelligences (Gardner 1999) (see Figure 2–2).

Group Norms

Group, or class, norms is a friendlier phrase than class rules, which is understood by teachers and students to mean Teacher's Rules. Allowing students to negotiate acceptable and unacceptable classroom behaviors, based on what supports or impedes learning, means that they will be held accountable for supporting a learning environment. "Community," according to Wolk, "is not just a place to live but an active way to live together" (2003, 57). When we connect class rules to learning, students respond more favorably. There's a reason for the rules that they can relate to.

The first year my students established the class norms I wanted to be very democratic. As a result, each of the five classes I taught that semester established different norms, which I then posted around the room. All classes agreed that the classroom should support learning, that homework needed to be completed as assigned, and that no one be allowed to disrupt another person's learning or use put-downs. All of the important rules I would have invoked were there.

While the norms for each class were substantially the same, there were some differences. These primarily involved the volume and type of background music allowed, the number of trips to the bathroom permitted each week, and the parameters for acceptable or unacceptable food (usually determined by the smell factor) allowed to be consumed during class. By the end of the third day I was thoroughly confused. Which class could eat French fries and which had to have soft rock playing in the background? Which class agreed to one bathroom break and which said one student out on a pass at a time? Then I got smarter.

I told the classes that I needed to avoid confusion and create an environment that had uniform norms since I was in the room all day. I removed all the posters and rewrote the norms as one class set governing all five teaching periods. There were no complaints. No one seemed to

Establishing Learning Communities Exercise

Instructions (to students): Think of a time in your school career when you have had powerful learning experiences. Think of times when you have not learned well. Complete the following sentences.

1. I learn best when
    a.
    b.
    c.
    d.
    e.

2. I don't learn well when
    a.
    b.
    c.
    d.
    e.

In your small group, present one of the conditions that support learning. Continue until everyone's ideas have been expressed. Repeat for those factors that impede learning. Create a single group list, in descending order, of those conditions that were most frequently cited. Determine the five conditions your group believes are essential for promoting academic success. List five conditions that the group agrees definitely impede learning. Prepare to discuss these factors when we establish class norms.

FIGURE 2–2 Establishing Learning Communities Exercise

notice that I had altered a few, softening the edges to maximize the positive and reduce the impediments to learning. In subsequent semesters we did the same exercise, compiled the optimum conditions for each class, and then I wrote the final list of class norms based on the student input. There is power in being the recording secretary; the written norms become the collective memory.

Once the norms are established and posted, any infractions become an infraction of students' rules, not the teacher's. For instance, the student who continually gets out of his seat and wanders about the room is violating the class norm of remaining seated unless you have a reason to move about—much more democratic than rules I see that say no getting out of your seat. Gently reminding the misbehaving student while pointing to the wall poster is usually enough to stop a distracting behavior; ditto for boisterous talking or playing music too loudly.

Lifelong Learning

Learning has to start with the teacher. Stretch yourself constantly and share those stretches with your students. Take a moment to talk about a book you're reading, a workshop you've attended, an advanced degree you're seeking. If you are working toward National Board Certification, engage your students in your pursuit. Wonder aloud. Ask a question and have your class become researchers along with you seeking the answer. I once brought the books from my nightstand to class. I amazed myself by the variety of things I was reading and the different reasons I had for reading magazines, fiction and nonfiction, research articles, reviews, a few newspapers I hadn't finished, and professional journals. My nightstand reading led to a discussion about why we read and study and how we move from being students of a teacher and curriculum to being self-motivated learners. It became a valuable teaching moment.

"Today, the estimate is that graduates of our schools leave knowing perhaps 2 percent of what they will need to know in the years ahead— 98 percent is yet to come. We all know the figures: knowledge doubles every three years; computer technology changes in eighteen months; the borders of Russia won't hold still. Yet today's graduates leave high school knowing far more than they ever did back in the fifties. The notion that we can acquire once and for all a basic kit of knowledge that will hold us in good stead for the rest of our lives is folly" (Barth 2001). Helping your students to become lifelong learners, capable of learning what they need in the years ahead, begins with you as a model.

Emotional Safety

Many of our students have had positive learning experiences at home and in school. They enter the classroom expecting to be liked and respected. They come ready to learn whatever it is you have to teach. But when a child comes to the classroom with a history of failure and negative emotional experiences, she has learned that she is not valued or respected and that the teacher and classroom are unsafe. She expects to fail, you may expect her to fail, and she behaves accordingly—she fails. Students who have not been successful in the past are afraid to try. They reason that if they try their hardest and are still not successful, then it must be because they are dumb. But if they don't try hard and they are not successful they can say they are smart, they just didn't try. We have to make it safe to try.

Alfee Enciso, a National Board Certified English language arts teacher, does it right. He is continually taking academic risks in his own work, trying new strategies, inviting other teachers to observe and critique him, and submitting articles he writes to local newspapers and professional journals. He celebrates his students' academic risk taking as well. Prominently displayed on one wall in his classroom is a sign, "Failure Bulletin Board." There students post work that is in process, that hasn't quite reached the pinnacle but that demonstrates they're stretching beyond their own comfort zone. Sometimes there's a student's story or joke that bombed. Alfee keeps his rejection letters there as well. Students proudly display their work, because it's okay to be imperfect. In my yoga class, the teacher celebrates when we try a pose, push ourselves, and fall over. It's all about reaching beyond your current ability level because if you don't reach, you'll never grow. But if you don't feel emotionally safe, you'll never take the risk. That's the environment we have to provide in our classrooms.

It's not that difficult. It begins with genuinely caring about your students—teens in their formative years. It's an atmosphere that doesn't allow put-downs, ever. It's being respectful and sensitive to students' beliefs. I learned most about what is important for a positive classroom environment from my students' journals. One year a female student wrote that she really appreciated that I didn't allow anyone to curse, even what we would consider mild cursing, in class. In her home no one cursed and it was very disturbing to her when she heard offensive language in class. One might assume because of all the foul language in movies, in rap music, even overheard in the school cafeteria that all teens curse, but that's just not so. Make your classroom a haven from outside negative forces. Begin with yourself.

Win-Win Atmosphere

In a learning community there is no need for classroom competition. Everyone can master the instructional and behavioral goals, given sufficient time, adequate scaffolding, and appropriate effort. If you have traditionally employed a bell-curve grading system, ask why and what purpose it serves.

Grading a paper with a red F sends a very different message than writing, "This work is not yet ready for a grade." In the former instance, the student didn't master the skill or task and isn't permitted or expected to try again. In the latter, the work is in progress, needs to be revised and resubmitted. I wish I could report that every student who receives a *not yet ready* will actually revise and redeem himself, but that would be deceitful. While all students do have the opportunity to resubmit their work, only some students actually do. For these students there is significant academic progress. But there's no progress when you write a red "Fail" across the face of their work.

There's another message inherent in the *not yet ready* approach, it's *I'm sticking with you until you master this goal or skill. I believe in you and I will be there to help you to succeed. I'm not quitting on you and you don't get to quit on yourself either.* Instead of *You didn't make it,* the message is, *What do we need to do (together) to help you to be successful?* It's likely that you still won't reach all of the students, but even moving one student closer to success is worth the effort—and there's not much effort required. As a nation we can't afford to toss away any of our children.

Celebrate

Celebrate everything. Birthdays, passing the driving test, using a credit card for the first time, turning in an assignment, not fighting with your mom or your best friend, or saying good riddance to a poorly chosen boy- or girlfriend. Celebrate the serious and the frivolous, but celebrate. Avoid competition in the celebrations. That doesn't mean that you don't have a bulletin board, as I did, to celebrate "best work," but it does mean that everyone knows they can make the board, it's about effort and applying effective strategies and not settling for less than you're capable of doing.

Celebrating is about honoring passages: first times, last times, special events. It's another way of honoring the whole child. When you celebrate a parent's recovery, a new house, learning to roller blade or gaining skill on a skate board, you acknowledge the child is more than their test scores. You also allow space for every child. Find something to celebrate, help the child to identify events to celebrate. Maybe it's arriving to school on time three days in a row, having the dog not eat your homework, avoiding dessert because you're trying to fit into the prom dress you deliberately bought one size too small.

Celebrate random acts of kindness in order to promote thinking and doing random acts of kindness.

Time

Last, but maybe most important, create a sense of space and time in your classroom. We don't have to have a dispatch on the board every day. There are times when we need to come into class and talk, or just be, or think about what happened during the day that has already passed. We need time to think about our learning. Take a few minutes to write in a journal about what you've learned, or to tell a classmate, or to tell the class. One of the most startling insights I gained was after asking students to write in their journals on a Friday afternoon something they had learned that week. Everyone wrote immediately and continued to write until I asked for pens down. That everyone wrote, that no one had nothing to say, was in itself startling. When we went around the room to share what we'd written, only two students talked about what they had learned in our English language arts class—a reminder that most of their learning happens outside of the classroom, even outside of school. Children are sponges, observing and learning from our behavior, from what is said and what is not said, from one another, from their parents and from TV and the media. The curriculum accounts for only about 17 percent of all learning.

Allow time for thinking and talking about learning. In this very frenetic, stressful world we live in, slow the pace down on occasion. Allow for wait time after asking questions. In our rush to cover the mandated curriculum, to keep pace with the pacing plan, we often forget that we also need time for thinking about our learning, for goal setting, for evaluating our own progress. Make your classroom a haven that respects time and how we use it; an escape from the hurly-burly, nonstop, bell-ringing school schedule where every time the bell rings we change hats, comply with new rules, experience new stresses. We need time for thinking, for just being. Planned silence can be golden.

Classroom Culture

You can create a classroom culture that supports high-quality, continuous learning. The culture is a reflection of the traditions, norms, attitudes, beliefs, behaviors, values, ceremonies, and myths that are ingrained in the current class, and in your long-term reputation at the school.

Ken Robinson writing in *Out of Our Minds,* quotes David Liddle of Interval Research,

> A creative organization . . . has several fundamental characteristics: It is first and foremost a place that gives people freedom to take risks; second, it is a place that allows people to discover and develop their own natural intelligence; third, it is a place where there are no "stupid" questions and no "right" answers; and fourth, it is a place that values irreverence, the lively, the dynamic, the surprising, the playful. (2001, 193)

Strive to make your classroom a "creative organization" where diversity leads to more creativity. I believe there will be a resurgence in the value we place on progressive, constructivist education that will move us away from restrictive thinking and knowledge-based testing. You don't have to wait; your classroom can help students to achieve academic success without abandoning the joy inherent in learning.

Pause and Reflect

We don't learn by doing, we learn by thinking about what we're doing.

Sketch out your current classroom configuration so you can study it, or sit in your classroom after everyone has left for the day and look around. How does it feel? Is there space for growing and stretching our minds? Do students have access to resources? Is it a place where you want to be? What changes can you make to create a physical space conducive to learning? What improvements within yourself will you make?

Begin a learning journal for yourself, for your students. Take a few moments at the end of the day to think about what you've learned—about your students, about the world, about your subject areas, about yourself.

Chapter Three

Motivation

When Teachers Care, Students Will Follow

All students want to learn. Every day they enter your classroom with the expectation that they will learn something. But motivating them to learn what we've set out for them is another issue entirely. Because "unmotivated students will probably do poor work or no work, learn little, and often exhibit irresponsible or disruptive behaviors" (Erwin 2003, 19), motivating them becomes critical to an active, powerful teaching and learning experience. This is not startling news to any secondary teacher.

So what to do about unmotivated students? There's a great deal you can do, and points and stars aren't it. Motivation increases only temporarily, and only for a few, when we provide external rewards. External rewards work best on lower-order skills, not on higher-order ones like critical thinking.

Just watch those same students you're saying are not motivated when they are in another teacher's room, or practicing on a skateboard, or spending hours primping their hair. We sometimes mistake their unenthusiastic response to our teaching or to the curriculum as lack of interest in learning, but we couldn't be more wrong.

Motivation increases dramatically when the right conditions exist. And the teacher is responsible for setting those conditions.

Students need:

- An orderly, secure, pleasant environment in order to learn (Erwin 2003; Goleman 1995). Establishing a classroom environment that supports learning begins with your belief about students and their ability to learn.

- To feel like they are cared about. If you can't love them, you're in the wrong profession. You can't even be lukewarm; you have to be hot on kids.

- To feel like they belong to the community of learners. Every student has something of value to contribute. Sometimes we have to dig a little deeper to find it, but it's worth the effort.

- To feel powerful. "Power means personal growth; developing knowledge and skills that increase the quality of our lives, lead us to achieve, and increase our feeling of self-worth" (Erwin 2003, 106). Feelings of power come from being able to do—from competence, not false praise, meaningless points, or inflated grades.

- Time to be successful. How much time and guidance do students have to explore their work and their problems with it? Do you allow for wait time, time for students to retrieve information, before you move onto another student or ask a second question? Do you allow time for students to develop interpersonal relationships, to meet and get to know one another before tackling a group project? We learn in a social context. Do you honor this?

- Choice. Ask yourself, what role does choice play in my classroom? Does the task have to be done in only one way—your way? Where is having choice more conducive to learning than not having choice would be? Do you regularly model the strategies that students need to shape their projects to their own interests and concerns and that allow students to make good choices?

- Relevance. Lack of motivation frequently centers around this. If students are not able to make connections between what you want them to learn and what they perceive they need to know, motivation will be low. Hold regular discussions about the value of the curriculum to students' current and future lives. If you can't find any value in part of the curriculum, what can you do to substitute something else or minimize the time spent on that which is valued less? Consider adding a service-learning component if you don't already have one. Contributing to the community helps students feel powerful and relevant and important.

- **Redemption.** Allow second and third chances to demonstrate learning. The portfolio provides a perfect vehicle for revision and redemption. Allow students time to select and reflect on work they haven't mastered, and then to redo the work to redeem themselves.

- **Freedom.** Although I don't advocate anarchy, I do allow students the easy freedoms, like choosing one's own seat, selecting group members for major projects, or having a variety of ways to demonstrate accomplishment.

- **To be free from** boring, repetitive, irrelevant work delivered in the same manner day in and day out. Surprise them, and yourself, by employing a variety of strategies, by changing the seating, by varying the routine sometimes. Boredom is actually "a form of depression—a kind of anger turned inward; and a longing for that which will transform the self, making life and learning meaningful" (Strong et al. 2003). I'm more likely to feel bored if I don't believe I can learn what you're asking me to learn. For example, when I say I find math boring, what I'm really saying is that I find it very difficult, I feel like I'll never make it so why try, and I stop listening; I check out mentally. Begin from where the student has mastery, even if that means returning to primary numeracy or literacy, and build from there. You don't have to do it alone, either. Engage fellow teachers and school personnel, parents, other students, and the students themselves.

- **Fun.** Think of fun in terms of pleasure, enjoyment, and laughter. "Fun is a by-product of having friends (love and belonging), being successful (power), having autonomy (freedom), and feeling safe and secure (survival)" (Erwin 2003, 20). That old axiom about not smiling until March should be tossed out with the first chalk dust of the semester. Laugh loudly and laugh often. Laugh at yourself, with your students, with the joy and excitement of learning.

- **An advocate.** If the mandated policies are not working for your students, or are actually working against them, gather your evidence and advocate for change. Too much of what happens in schools is for and about the adult agenda, not the students' needs. Say not, "They'll never let us," instead ask, "What is it that I believe constitutes a good education for these youngsters? And how am I going to enlist resources to change this school [my classroom] so that we can provide that education?" (Barth 2001, 10).

- Motivation is highest when teachers and schools care about kids.

Pause and Reflect

Are your students engaged? How do you assist students in gaining personal power? In making good decisions? Perhaps more important, are you engaged in your teaching and personal learning? If not, how can you become engaged? If so, what works for you and how can you supplement that?

Chapter Four

Beginning with the End in Mind

A Case for Why the End Is the Beginning

"Would you tell me please which way I ought to walk from here?" "That depends a good deal on where you want to get to," said the Cat. "I don't much care where," said Alice. "Then it doesn't matter which way you walk," said the Cat.

■Lewis Carrol, *Alice's Adventures in Wonderland*

Classrooms "that nurture apathy and passiveness in children help propagate apathy and passiveness in society" (Wolk 1998, viii). Our secondary classrooms are filled with Alices who don't much care where they are going and who graduate and become citizens who don't much care. Ask yourself, "what kind of neighbors [you] want, what kind of community [you] want, what kind of nation [you] want, what kind of world [you] want" (Wolk 1998) and then teach with that end in mind.

Instructional Goals—Academic Content Standards

I am a fervent supporter of academic content standards, although I reserve the right as a mindful teacher to thoughtfully select standards for my students. They define and shape what we teach and what students are expected to learn. Used conscientiously standards can be beacons guiding teachers and students in their quest for academic excellence. Standards are anything but standard; how students demonstrate accomplishment can be as different as the students themselves.

To use the content standards in a meaningful way you have to know the standards for your subject and grade levels as well as those standards students should have achieved before coming to your class. Additionally, you need to know what students are expected to know and be able to do to be successful in their subsequent classes and for life beyond the classroom. And the students need to know also.

What Students Will Know and Be Able to Do

I begin each semester's or year's course with a discussion around the instructional goals—a term I much prefer to standards. "At the end of this semester, or year," I tell the students, "you're going to be able to communicate your ideas in writing and orally to a variety of audiences. You'll know how to persuade people, how to get them emotionally involved, to care about what you have to say. You'll be able to back up your opinions because you'll know how to research and gather evidence to support and challenge your beliefs and others'. You'll be more effective readers, so no one will ever be able to swindle you by saying one thing while having written something else in the contract you sign to buy that house or car or to enter that partnership. You'll know how to explore a text, fiction or nonfiction, and find meaning and relevance for your lives. And you'll have skills that are valued in the marketplace and in society. You'll be creative risk takers who push the current boundaries of science and math and technology and much more." My opening-day speech varies with the audience of students, connecting with ideas they value and situations they are likely to meet. I introduce the why of our learning before I introduce the academic standards.

Contrast this speech, focused on the *what* and the *why* of study, with one that begins with rules and points needed to earn grades. Your passion and commitment about the work you're doing is contagious. Hook your students in. Invite them to join you on this exciting learning journey.

I spend a great deal of my preparation time studying the state content standards. I begin with the assumption that lots of talented educators, and others, carefully selected the standards we want our students to achieve. I may disagree with some emphasis, but on the whole I find merit in them. As a masterful, mindful teacher I reserve the right to determine how I'm going to help students to achieve those standards. I come to the classroom with a deep understanding of how we can apply the mandated content standards to the goals we've set for our own teaching and learning. The standards don't mandate how I am to teach to them, or even what resources I should use. There is great flexibility for me to select the most appropriate materials and strategies, and for students to exercise choice in demonstrating accomplishment. And when school policy seeks to limit the flexibility I need to meet all of my students' needs, I gather evidence of my teaching and students' learning in the form of portfolios and I continue to teach so all of my students can learn.

Student-Friendly Standards

Although mine is a standards-based classroom, I never post the state standards as written. The published standards are guides for teachers, not intended to be posted on the wall as a guide for the students—in spite of what some administrators may demand. Along with my department colleagues, we've squeezed the standards, pulled out the common themes, and converted them to student-friendly language. (See Chapter Six.) From the very outset *students know where we're going and why we're going there*. We spend more time talking about the why then we spend on the what.

Our English Language Arts standard (this is the rewritten version, not the state published standard) is as follows: *Consistently and properly use the conventions of standard written and spoken English.* The why is about communicating our ideas to the reader or listener. Because we have discussion around the purpose of the conventions, when I comment on student essays I can say, "I'm confused by your use of this comma, can you explain its use?" I send students to the grammar section of their anthology and ask them to explain their punctuation marks or to remove or alter them. I don't have to reteach the use of the comma, which they've been studying since third grade, the rules of which they may be lazily applying. *When students know you are going to do the correcting, they don't have to take responsibility for using the conventions correctly in the first place.* Return the responsibility to the students.

Identifying the semester or yearlong instructional goals and then getting student buy-in requires spending some up-front time. You need to know the standards well, have applications that are meaningful and relevant for your current student population, and then teach to those standards so students can achieve them at high levels. Low expectations result in lowered achievement, disengagement, and boredom. In national studies the Ed Trust, a Washington, DC based think tank, found over and over again that secondary students did not feel challenged. They said they could do much more than they were doing, but no one asked. We can't be lulled into thinking they can only do less because they do less. There is the appearance of apathy because we don't challenge them enough.

Establishing and conveying the goals in advance engages students as partners in their own learning. If they don't know where they are going, they won't know which road to take nor will they be able to assess their progress. Allowing for choice whenever possible increases engagement.

Backward Design

Grant Wiggins and Jay McTighe use the term *backward design:* "identify desired result; determine acceptable evidence; plan learning experiences and instruction" (1998, 8). Although I certainly agree with the Wiggins-McTighe emphasis on designing instruction based on the instructional goals, as originally conceived backward design is done by the teacher with results delivered to the student. For students to become shapers of their own worlds, they need to also be part of the backward-design process. In an ideal setting, we would negotiate the instructional goals together. Unfortunately because time is limited and because students enter our classes with varying degrees of experience, skills, and interests, goal setting from scratch with students may not be practical or efficient. The next best procedure is for the teacher (department) to select the targeted standards and to convince the students why attaining the standards is in their own best interest. We convince them through reasoning, through knowing their interests and current knowledge and skills, and by conveying the ever-changing requirements of the world beyond the classroom.

Differentiation

Having all the students do the same assignments at the same time is not about equality, it's about convenience. It's also about assuming that when we have a standardized input, the output (what each student knows and is able to do) is also standardized. That just doesn't work, and teaching to the standards doesn't mean that student output will be identical. In the hands of a skilled teacher, standards are anything but standard.

By beginning with the end in mind and thinking in terms of individual students who monitor their own learning, all students can have the same instructional goals—the skills and knowledge they will need to be successful in their next setting (academic or otherwise). Each works toward accomplishment beginning with what they know and can do.

Some students come to your class already having met the grade-level standards. You can help these students to go deeper, to expand what they know, by using the skills they've previously acquired. Others come less prepared, for a variety of reasons, frequently including low expectations from previous teachers; lack of serious prior effort on their part to achieve; or social promotion, which may have done much for their self-esteem but little to motivate them to apply themselves. Given the goals in advance, students will need to demonstrate that they have met or exceeded those goals in order to be successful in the course.

Setting the Standard

At the beginning of a semester goal-setting session with newly arrived ninth graders, several heads nodded in agreement when I said that some of them had gotten by without doing much of anything for a long time. This year, I advised them, they wouldn't move on unless they could provide *clear, consistent, and convincing* evidence of their learning. That meant that those who may not have worked to their full potential in the past might have a lot of catching up to do. I assured them that I would stay with them, provide lots of opportunities to achieve the instructional goals, and allow for multiple revisions and eventual redemption. There would be additional opportunities to succeed through after-school tutoring programs, in Saturday school classes, and through their own increased efforts. What there wouldn't be was any hiding out or sliding by.

Begin with the End Goal and Make It Relevant

In preparation for the course(s) you're teaching, first consider what you want students to know and be able to do by the end of their time with you. Although you may use the published state or district content standards as your guide, you still have to make the standards your own. If you don't believe the state/district standards are important goals for your students to meet, then you'll never be able to convince students of their importance and they in turn won't expend their time or effort to achieve them. Students care more about you, their teacher, than they do about some standards printed in a state framework.

For each instructional goal you select, be prepared to identify multiple nonacademic applications. If you can't figure out why an algebraic algorithm you're teaching is important, don't be surprised if students don't get it, or don't retain it, or can't apply it. We learn and retain what is meaningful and relevant and we discard the rest. This is the reasoning behind the opening speech I give each year. I strive to convince students that what we're studying really is relevant and important for each of them. I strengthen my argument with examples I keep current. Whenever possible, I include references to local community events. It's all about relevance.

Examining a host of "beyond the classroom" applications for each instructional goal leads to selecting strategies that guide students as they achieve those goals. Because at the time they exit from high school students will know only about 2 percent of what they will need to know during their lifetime, it's important that we teach students how to learn (Barth 2001, 16). When we incorporate as part of the strategies we use in class the skills that are valued in the workplace, we set our students up for long-term success.

Essential Skills for the Twenty-First Century

I have had and continue to have many epiphanies in my teaching career. One came from a newspaper article in which futurist Peter Schwartz predicted that available information would double by the year 2020. I've since read that Schwartz had underestimated; information is doubling every three years and computer technology changes in eighteen months (Barth 2001)! If that is the case, then what are we teaching students now that will be important and meaningful when they enter adulthood as parents, as citizens, as part of the workforce? How can we teach for a future we can't even define? How can we not?

Those questions led me on another quest during which I found David Thornburg's work: *The New Basics: Education and the Future of Work in the Telematic Age* (Thornburg 2002). Thornburg identifies twenty-first-century core skills as: (1) Digital-Age Literacy—including cultural literacy and global awareness; (2) Inventive Thinking—being able to adapt and take risks, curiosity and creativity, and sound reasoning and higher-order thinking; (3) Effective Communication—"teaming, collaboration, and interpersonal skills" as well as "personal and social responsibility"; and (4) High Productivity—the "ability to prioritize, plan, and manage . . . [and to] create relevant, high-quality products" (59). I use Thornburg's core skills as the foundation of my teaching practice, especially as I select strategies.

While I build these skills into the curriculum through group projects, authentic communication assignments, open-ended problem solving, high expectations, varied audiences for student work, multimedia resources, and time for reflecting about learning, it is essential to involve the students from the outset. We begin the year talking about each of Thornburg's core skills, thinking about jobs that rely heavily on these skills, interviewing parents and relatives about the skills they use, and doing research into careers. Then, during the year, as we incorporate particular strategies, I refer to the core skills and point out how these strategies move us toward achieving them. In this way the work we do in class has multiple layers of meaning; the what, why, and how of our learning.

You may question the relevance of these strategies in an English language arts class. I would reply that I teach students, not curriculum. As we read literature during the year, we sometimes stop and discuss what skills the characters needed to be successful in their culture during their time, and compare those skills to what we need today. I ask students whether they can learn from other times and places and people. They usually answer that there are some things to be learned from the past, other things for which we need to explore the present (including contemporary writers), and still others that require probing into the future. This is also reflected in their portfolios, which include the curriculum goals, the academic habits of mind, and Thurnburg's core skills for the twenty-first century. (For more on portfolios, see Chapter Six.)

Mandated Assessments

Okay, you're thinking, this is all well and good, but in an era of mandated assessments, pacing plans, and standardized tests the goals have already been clearly defined; you are required to teach to those. And you can, with some personalized touches—if you begin with the end in mind.

At several of the districts where I consult, the teachers in each core department (science, math, language arts, and social studies/history) are now required to administer periodic assessments to all students in each class. The stated purpose is to make certain that everyone is teaching the same curriculum, and that students, should they transfer, are not at a disadvantage. While I vehemently disagree with the controlling premise, and have not found any valid education studies to support this mandate, I understand the perceived need to comply. Here's how: begin with the end in mind.

Examine the assessment prompt (test, assignment) or one similar to the actual prompt if it is not released in advance. Analyze: What are the core skills a student must have achieved in order to be successful on this assessment? What is the basic knowledge it covers? Then, start your learning sequence with what the students will have to accomplish, minus what they already know. If they will need to demonstrate a business letter, incorporate business-style letters for authentic reasons. Guide students as they select an appropriate topic of interest to them and have them write to their congressmen, to scientists working on genetics research, or to corporate executives making decisions about outsourcing, for example. For an assessment on friendly-letter format, write some friendly letters. When a ninth-grade class of English language learners was asked to write to service men and women in Afghanistan, they wrote pages filled with details about their own lives and asked about the soldiers' lives; they asked questions about the war, about living conditions, about the people of Afghanistan. And when the soldiers wrote back, students wrote again, asking about opportunities in the military, about hobbies, and about family left behind. Did they learn letter-writing format? Absolutely. They also learned a bit about English vocabulary and grammar. They learned about the military, about Afghanistan, about democracy and its benefits. They knew their letters would be read by more people than the teacher, so they took more care—exactly what you want them to do when they take standardized tests. All the while, they were preparing for the mandated assessment, on which they did very well.

Pacing Plans

If your curriculum is driven by a mandated pacing plan, breathe deeply and begin with the end in mind. All pacing plans have in common the stipulation that by such and such a date students will have covered this curriculum—as if anyone could mandate what students will learn and how quickly. Instead of taking the pacing plan step-by-step and hoping you get through the entire curriculum in spite of special schedules, absenteeism, and public address announcements that interrupt teaching, begin with the big ideas. A pacing plan I reviewed for a high school integrated science class listed 12.6 days for one of the units. Even the science teacher laughed when I asked him how he determined a ".6 teaching day" (some pacing plans I've reviewed divide the lessons into fractions of periods but don't indicate how the allocated time period is determined) and what to do if a student asks an unexpected and highly interesting question that was not part of the pacing plan. I suspect that when we focus on student learning, pacing plans will be abandoned, or at least altered considerably to allow space and time for students to learn. In the meantime, I'll work with them and remain focused on students.

Pacing plans and mandated assessments are more about teaching and adult agendas then they are about learning and students. Here's where a masterful teacher makes critical decisions. First ask, what are those concepts and skills students should be familiar with by when? Then teach those. Take the time to go into depth about a few ideas rather than try to cover everything superficially. Research from the University of Wisconsin found that students who were assigned more demanding intellectual work scored about 50 percentile points higher on authentic measures of student achievement. "Assignments that don't go beyond reproducing information, such as filling in the blanks, wouldn't prepare students for intellectual challenges posed by the modern workplace and by civic and personal affairs" (Rosenbaum 2001).

Take Risks

In this era of strangling mandates, standardized tests, and pacing plans you still need to be an advocate for learning. That's why you teach. When you do stray from the requirements, keep records—in the form of student portfolios—about student learning, and then close the door. As long as students are learning at high levels and are engaged in rigorous curriculum, you can feel satisfied that you are making the right decisions.

Standardized Tests

Standardized tests have many features in common. In addition to the content focus, usually spelled out in advance because the district wants your students to do well, there are also test-taking strategies that incorporate vocabulary specific to the test directions—words like *explain, choose, define, list, greater or less than*, and so on. Instead of taking time to complete worksheets focused on test taking, incorporate these words and strategies into your curriculum throughout the year. Tell students what you're doing and why. Make your teaching transparent. "We're doing this because . . ." or "This is important to learn now because you'll be tested in the spring," or "because in the workplace team work is highly valued."

Essential Understandings and Essential Questions

> An essential understanding represents a big idea having enduring value beyond the classroom. [Essential understandings] are umbrella-like organizers of what you want your students to remember thirty years from now—and longer!
>
> *http://magnet.sandi.net/workshops/informationquest/essential.html*

When you plan your learning sequences by identifying the big ideas first, then determine how to get students to a deep understanding of that big idea, you are planning with the end in mind.

1. In planning essential understandings, ask yourself:

- What do I want my students to understand about this topic?
- What big ideas do I want my students to understand beyond this topic?

2. It is often helpful to begin with "Students understand that . . ." and complete the sentence with two or more concepts from your standards or unit of study (Erikson 1998).

3. Be sure to write your essential understandings in kid-friendly language so all your students can understand what they will be learning.

An *essential question* represents the essence of what your students will examine and learn in the course of their study (Perkins-Gough 2003). Essential questions promote deep and enduring understanding. They cannot be answered in one sentence. When writing essential questions:

1. Create a reasonable number, one or two per lesson, and between three and five for a unit of study that ranges from three to twelve weeks.

2. Frame your questions in kid-friendly language. Make them engaging and provocative. (Use the KWL strategy to guide students in framing their own questions.)

3. Design questions that reflect the standards and big ideas of your content area. These questions should have substance and power and require a number of activities that engage the students in an investigation.

4. If a question is too specific, or could be answered with a few words or a sentence, it is probably not an essential question.

5. Write essential questions with "how" or "why" instead of "what."

6. Sequence your questions so one leads naturally to another.

7. Post these questions in your room as a learning focus for your students.

The examples that follow are loosely paraphrased from multiple websites, teacher discussions, and personal experience. The referenced standards are from the California State Frameworks (1999):

> *English Language Arts Standard*: The student understands, analyzes, interprets, evaluates, and extends the meaning of a wide variety of significant literature—nonfiction, fiction, poetry, and drama. *Essential understanding*: Students understand that an author's point of view, word choice, content, and style can influence or change readers' opinions about a subject. *Essential questions*: In her book *Silent Spring*, Rachel Carson warned us of the dangers of using pesticides like DDT and how dangerous this chemical is to both animals and people. How did her point of view, scientific information, and writing style impact our society's awareness of this problem? What is the continuing impact, if any? Were there unexpected consequences of paying more attention to the effects of pesticides? If so, what are they?

> *Math Standard*: The student uses ratios and proportional reasoning to convert within measurement systems. *Essential understanding*: Students understand that measurement skills have real life applications. *Essential questions*: If you could redecorate your house anyway you wanted, how much carpeting, linoleum, paint, or wallpaper would you need to buy? How much would these materials cost?

Science Standard: The student develops an understanding of life and the flow of matter and energy in ecosystems. *Essential understandings*: Matter and energy are transferred from one organism to another in an ecosystem. Organisms have specific roles in an ecosystem. *Essential questions*: Everybody needs food to survive. In the kelp forest you could end up as somebody's dinner if you are low on the food chain. How are matter and energy transferred from one organism to another within a kelp forest? If you were a California sheepshead living in a kelp forest, how would you make a living?

Ask yourself, what's really important for the students to garner from this learning sequence? What big ideas do I want my students to understand beyond this immediate topic? Do you want them to understand, as I did in one learning sequence about point of view, that literature and history and every text, including the newspaper, has a point of view; that it's nearly impossible to be totally objective and unbiased; that it's important to recognize the author's bias? What is *not* an essential understanding is merely to complete the chapter and answer the questions at the end.

Elaine Johnson, writing in *Contextual Teaching and Learning*, states that "from electron to galaxy, the entire universe is sustained and ordered by three principles, those of interdependence, differentiation, and self-organization" (2002, 26). Teaching through this lens opens the way to studying relationships (animals to plants, individuals to groups, the past to the present), how we are different and the same (comparison-contrast, diversity of species and ethnic groups, complexity and variation), and how we sustain ourselves (evolution, self-actualization, government systems). The variations are endless. The end goal is to employ various lenses through which to study the world, make order from chaos, and attach academic learning to daily life. I haven't come across a topic I couldn't examine through these lenses. Interdependence, differentiation, and self-organization are essential understandings.

Just as each author and each reader has a point of view, so does each student. You may think you are teaching the same content to everyone in your class, but the reality is that because students are different from one another, with different prior knowledge, they will receive different information and cull different concepts from the same lesson. We teach individual students, but we do that in group settings. Change the composition of the group and you alter the learning. Provide for group and individual project-based work and students will grow—in their social context and as self-actualized beings.

Shared Inquiry

The mind naturally seeks answers. We turn our students into learning machines when we help them formulate questions and then seek answers. Here are some examples of shared inquiry: Suppose your students are reading the story of Jack and the Beanstalk. Reading with a question in mind, *Does Jack succeed because of his luck or because of his ability?* pushes students to seek out details, to form opinions, to make predictions, draw conclusions, and to be generally more engaged than if they are reading the same story for sequence of events or even for theme.

You might begin discussing Jack's luck versus his ability, then move on to Donald Trump. Is he financially successful because he was born rich? Got lucky? Took risks? Played the media well? There isn't a secondary student who doesn't know about Trump—his books, his TV shows (*The Apprentice*), his buildings, and personal life—and wouldn't want to get some answers. And by the way, how do we measure success? How do you measure it for yourself? What great themes to explore!

Here's another inquiry question: *When we purchase sports shoes, what are the effects on the global economy, on the environment, on third-world development, on media?* There's enough depth in this question to guide a semester-long study of history, economics, government, ecology, ethics, and media.

And still another: *It is said that democracy is the best system of government. Best for whom? Better than what?* And yet another: *What is the impact of wiping out even one plant or animal species? Why should we care?*

Here's one I used when reading the opening chapters of Yann Martel's novel *Life of Pi*: *Are zoos a benefit or impediment to wild animal life on this planet? Support your opinion with evidence from the text, from personal experience, from other resources* (Martel 2003).

English teacher Ron Harris of Monroe High School in Los Angeles is working on this inquiry question to guide his Expository Composition course: *Each generation is recognized by music developed and extolled during that decade or those decades. Fifty years in the future what music will be associated with the current times and why? Will the music favorably or unfavorably compare to the music of other eras? What criterion should one use for this comparison and why?*

We will ask students to bring the lyrics of songs they are attached to. They will also compare song lyrics to poems, past and contemporary, and to other lyrics. They will choose a movie, select and play ten minutes of the video and persuade others why this is the best movie of the decade. They will look for figurative language. They will write lyrics that capture a moment in time, or an entire generation. But the hook will be the lyrics they bring—every student will be motivated. This is actually a teacher-friendly unit because the students do most of the work. We'll read nonfiction about how to get into the recording industry, the role the media and money play in getting a song aired, the historical perspective of blackballing, and more. This is rich ground, with many opportunities to write persuasively, to do research, to compare and contrast—all genres required for expository composition. Ron can address the state standards and help his students to accomplish them. During the unit he and I will continually assess student progress, alter the plan along the way as needed, and learn a great deal about our students and contemporary culture. Students will also become critics of their contemporary culture as they seek and select the lyrics and movies they believe define this generation and determine what will be valued fifty years from now. I'm already curious about what they will select. This is all about making connections and using authentic assessments to meet the standards and requirements of expository composition, and it's exciting.

I just read an article in the *New York Sunday Times*, titled "Not Funnies" by Charles McGrath, editor of the *New York Times Book Review*. He argues, "that for today's younger readers, graphic novels, with their slackerish antiheroes and visual appeal to the image-literate, are positioned to usurp the role that the novel once played in the culture and asks whether or not they are good enough to actually do so" (2004). I wonder how many of our veteran English language arts teachers would dare to incorporate a serious study of the graphic novel (comic book) in an American literature course. Editor McGrath said, "[I] actually had to train [my]self how to read them, and it was a while before I realized that I was also having a huge amount of fun." How often do teachers go out of their way to study a new genre? How often do they teach and reteach the same literature, or conduct the same experiment even when it no longer interests them, simply because they know the material? It's important that we don't simply rehash what has gone before, but that we provide opportunities for our students to use contemporary resources. After all, kids want to learn. "As humans, we all strive to increase our sense of mastery. We take delight in developing new competencies, and we have a stake in acquiring those skills that will earn the respect of others" (Strong et al. 2003). And kids are reading (five million copies of the Rowling books sold the first weekend they were on sale in the United States) all the time. If your students are not enthusiastic learners and readers, what can you do to foster that love of learning? How can you be a learner in your own classroom?

Inquiry questions can drive a single lesson, a unit, or the entire semester's work. Students can develop their own questions (see the KWL Strategy in Chapter Nine), which they then seek to answer. The idea behind shared inquiry is to seek answers together with your students that you don't already have. When we pose and seek the answers to questions of interest to us, we are more engaged and learn at higher levels.

Most questioning in school, about 85 percent, falls into the category of "known response" questions. That means that the teacher already knows the answer to the question before he or she asks it and that students know you know the answer. When you ask students known-response questions, their goal is not to understand or to learn something new and of interest, but to give teachers the answers they want—no wonder students are disengaged and discipline becomes a driving force. But when we focus discovery and learning around shared inquiry questions, we become learners together.

Shared-inquiry teaching is a natural for differentiated instruction. For questions you provide, student responses will vary. Students with greater academic skill give more in-depth answers or opinions, but all students are able to respond at least to their ability and effort level. When students generate their own inquiry questions, even students who are usually uninvolved may surprise you with the high level of effort they expend in seeking answers to their own questions and to their classmates'.

Here's another advantage of student-generated questions: you won't have to think them up, or pull them from prior studies, or do anything other than listen, help students frame their questions, assist with resources, and ask them more questions about their questions and the answers they are finding. Great inquiry questions may never get answered to everyone's satisfaction; they generate more questions for more inquiry and more study, which leads to more learning.

Closing Remarks

When I first meet with a school's faculty, we examine their needs, then write a plan for professional development over time. Sometimes faculty members will say, "Just tell me what to do." It's not that I don't want to, I can't. There's no magic formula, no absolutely foolproof key to student learning. There's no curriculum guide, no script to follow, no set of strategies that will meet every student's needs or address every mandate. Teachers need to be constantly mindful, continually reflecting on what they are doing and how their students are learning. "The specialist who cannot take the holistic view of the whole scene is no use at all" (Robinson 2001, 193). What I've presented above are the big concepts that guide great teaching.

So, where to begin preparing for a new school year, or course, or grade? Begin with the standards for your course and grade level. Examine the standards that come before and those that follow. Within the context of those standards, frame inquiry questions that are interesting to you. What questions have been rattling around in your head? When you read the paper, hear the news, or read a professional journal, what more do you want to know? How can you frame your questions so you can bring them into your classroom?

As I write this, I'm sitting in my sister's house in Palm Springs overlooking the golf course (someone has to do it). I'm wondering how building materials are selected for a desert environment where temperatures can exceed 120 degrees. Through this inquiry I can study environment, resources, geography, and cost factors. We could expand this inquiry to different parts of the world. Why do some African villages build conical housing units? Why does the Eastern United States rely on bricks for building while the Southwest uses stucco? For a culminating project students could decide where they want to live, and then design a dwelling to fit that environment. Just thinking about this idea piques my imagination and curiosity—an essential twenty-first-century requirement for success.

When my Heinemann editor and I began this project, we envisioned a book about classroom management. Throughout the months I've spent researching and writing this book, the whole idea of classroom management has been evading me. Classroom management is not separate from teaching, it's intricately interwoven with everything you do and say. When students are engaged, when there is a community of learners, the management part is seamless and invisible.

Pause and Reflect

1. If your class ran perfectly (however you define perfect), what would it look like? What would students be doing and learning? What and how would you be teaching? Is your idea along the lines of the Stepford Project? More like controlled chaos? Something in between? Beginning with the end in mind, what steps do you need to take to turn that imaginary classroom into reality?

Let your mind wander. What interests you? What are you curious about? What big inquiry questions can you bring to the classroom?

2. "Classrooms and curriculums must be interesting, intellectual, critical, creative, purposeful, communal, and highly relevant . . . Getting students genuinely interested in what they are doing in school develops good classroom relationships and learning" (Wolk 2003, 33). What do you do to get students genuinely interested in learning? What could you do better?

Chapter Five

Assessments

Why We Do What We Do and
How We Can Do It Better

A bad instructor can go through an entire quarter leaving absolutely nothing memorable in the minds of his class, curve out the scores on an irrelevant test, and leave the impression that some have learned and some have not. But if the grades are removed the class is forced to wonder each day what it's really learning.

■Robert M. Pirsig, *Zen and the Art of Motorcycle Maintenance*

Teachers spend an inordinate amount of time grading. We grade papers, projects, exams, labs, and performances because we've always graded them. We grade to sort out those kids who know and can do and those who don't or can't or won't. We grade students because colleges demand grades and because parents and students themselves want to know how they are doing. And we grade because school districts require us to enter one or two grades in the roll book per student per week. What do we do with all the grades? How do we use them to inform our teaching? To inform students about their learning?

Before you give your next assignment, think through the following questions:

- What are you assessing?
- Why are you assessing it?
- How are you assessing it?
- Does the assessment align with the instructional goal(s)?
- Is it the right assessment?
- Why are you assessing it this way?

And the really big questions:

- How will you use the information/data to inform the student?
- How will you use the information/data to inform your teaching?

The Big Assessment Questions

During lesson planning, after you've identified the instructional goals, it's time to plan for assessment. How will you and the students know when they have achieved their goals? How will you and the students measure their progress? What follows are some questions to consider as you plan instruction, assignments, and grading.

What are you asking students to do and why are you asking them to do it? Is the curriculum rigorous? Is it worthy of their time? Is there an immediate or long-term payoff? Can you articulate the *what* of your teaching and the *why*, in order to increase student engagement? Are the strategies you've chosen the right ones for these students and for the targeted goals? Do you vary the strategies? Are they interactive? Do they engage students?

Assessment is about measurement and evaluation. How do you measure student output? When is verbal feedback sufficient? When and what should you grade? How much weight do you allot to each assignment? On what criteria do you base your decision? Does the grading rubric distinguish between mastery, proficiency, and basic and below-basic accomplishment? How? Have you identified which skill(s) or information students need to know or be able to do and which are worth assessing? Does your assessment address the targeted skills and/or information?

Have you combined standards (instructional goals) and skills into one assessment in order to avoid isolating discrete skills? Are students expected to be able to synthesize information? To persuade an audience? To apply an algorithm to a word problem? How can you add additional components like writing, speaking, or reading to assignments? Is use of technology a regular component of your assessments? Have you built in "recognizing and rewarding creative output in appropriate ways, and avoiding an atmosphere of accountability that discourages taking risks or that stifles exploratory activities in the interests of short-term gain" (Robinson 2001, 182).

Have you informed the students in advance of what you are assessing and why? Once they are aware of the goal and how they will be measured, they can target and monitor their own progress.

What benefit will students derive from completing this assessment? Will it reinforce their learning? Will it expand their abilities? What is the benefit to students of assessing it? To your teaching?

And here are the questions we are least familiar with. How will I use the data I gather from this student assessment to inform my own teaching? What does the class set of work tell me about my instruction? About the strategies I selected? The resources I provided or identified?

Once the goals have been selected, the lessons taught, the student work collected, graded, and studied, take time to reflect on the body of work. What strategies improved student output? What were not as effective? What would you do differently next time you teach these goals? What would you do the same? If some students haven't achieved the goals, how will you continue the work without retaining those students who have?

Formative and Summative Assessment

Let's begin with some basics. There are two kinds of assessments, formative and summative. Formative assessments happen along the way, not just at the end of a lesson or unit or course. They can be formal or informal, graded or not graded. Formative assessments help make student learning visible to us and to them. They also inform us, and the students, about the next steps we need to take toward completion and achievement. Formative assessments include observing, listening, questioning— asking and answering. When we observe students at work and study students' work we learn more about what they know and can do, and can plan accordingly. When we listen closely during discussions, we are assessing students' reasoning, their depth of understanding; we uncover misconceptions and accomplishment. Don't beat yourself up if you've never thought in terms of formative assessments. Until I began studying how to look at student work to inform instruction, neither had I.

Formative and summative assessments yield the most benefit when we use them to teach students to assess their own progress, a skill that will serve them well throughout their lives. Setting goals, analyzing one's progress toward achieving those goals, and planning next steps put students in charge of their own learning.

Summative assessments measure what a student knows and is able to do at a particular moment in time. Because it's entirely possible that the student or you are having a bad day at the moment in time when they are taking a final exam, or giving a final speech, or demonstrating a final project, we want to avoid overdependence on summative assessments. If the assessment is poorly designed, or the instructions are confusing, or you haven't allowed sufficient time for completion, the conclusions you and the students draw will be inaccurate. By using a combination of formative and summative assessments, you can avoid a false reading of their abilities. This is why portfolios, which are a collection of student work over time rather than a snapshot at one point in time, are a better way to assess student gains.

Feedback

Prompt, constructive feedback is crucial. How prompt? Aim for forty-eight hours or less. Feedback can be formal or informal, written or verbal. Use voice and body language to express your interest in students' work. Use signs of approval; a thumbs-up speaks volumes. Statements like *good job*, *well done*, *way to go*, and *keep trying* are fine as far as they go. As you're moving around the room and checking that students are indeed working, those simple phrases encourage them to continue their efforts.

Feedback occurs in many forms, it's all around us. It occurs naturally in the form of approval or encouragement when we applaud a performance; when significant adults review student's work; when a poster or essay or photo of a science project gets posted on the bulletin board; or when we award a ribbon or other prize for good work.

Prescriptive feedback is more than cheerleading. It tells the student exactly what to do. *"Hold the brush this way." "Try adding first and then multiplying." "This spot could use some dialogue, what should your character say?" "You've poured too much compound and that may skew your results; reread the instructions and begin again."* Comments like *revise this*, or red X's indicating an incorrect answer don't provide direction. Students need to know how to revise, where to begin correcting errors. Without explicit directions you're likely to get a blank stare and the same work written in a neater hand, or a turned-off student. If there is no possibility of redemption (changing the grade) it's likely that students will not even bother to revise or correct the work.

Select something for correction that requires the student to stretch, but that is still within reach. If you ask for too much at once, you're liable to get nothing. And then reward their success.

Comment, verbally or in writing, on what the student did well. *"I loved the way you added an accent to Romeo's voice when you gave your speech." "When I read the sensory details I could almost smell the flower; I wonder what* it felt like." "*Thank you for recording all the steps in the math solution, I could follow your thinking exactly—here's where you put a plus instead of a minus.*" "*Your wrist is swinging in a perfect arc; now flex your knees at the same time.*" Praise that is specific, combined with an enthusiastic delivery, motivates students to continue working toward their highest level of possible achievement at this time. Once they have successfully achieved the first part of the task, the next step doesn't seem so daunting.

Limit yourself to two comments. I'm appalled at some of the things I did early in my teaching career. I used to put at least ten or fifteen comments and corrections on every student's paper. I'd spend all weekend grading and commenting, only to have students take one look at the grade and ignore the comments. When students revised their papers, they'd make the corrections I suggested and never look at other errors. When asked why not, they said, "You didn't correct it." That's when I understood that if I was doing all the work students took less and less responsibility and learned less. For them, revision and correction were about pleasing the teacher, doing what the teacher wants instead of caring about their own work and striving for mastery. A combination of prescriptive feedback and genuine enthusiasm is more effective than either strategy used alone.

Peer Editing and Correcting

Don't be the only source of feedback for students' work. Teach students to provide feedback for one another. A word of caution: looking at one another's work, offering constructive criticism and honest praise, requires modeling. Students, and many adults, don't know how to do this well. Giving constructive feedback is a skill you can, and should, teach. I like to use the Fish Bowl strategy to demonstrate collaborative feedback to improve student work. The setup is simple. Select four students, three to critique and comment on the presented work and one who volunteers his work to be examined by the rest of the group. Provide a protocol. You can download several different protocols from <*www.lasw.org*>. Each group needs a facilitator; you model that role.

The facilitator reviews the rules for the group—how much time for presentation, the time allocation and order in which each group member will comment, the nature of the comments. If you've already established norms for a successful learning community, refer to those. Remind students that no put-downs are allowed, and use Reflective Conversation Starters (see Chapter Nine). A sample protocol:

Assessments

- The presenting student shows her work. She begins by describing the assignment. (I especially like to listen to this part of the presentation, her words and expression, because they say a great deal about how clear my original instructions were, and whether a student found the assignment relevant and meaningful.)
- The presenting student discusses what she wants the others to comment on. It may be that she's working on dialogue, or converting word problems to numerical formulas, or writing her hypothesis in preparation for a science lab. Because comments without focus are not as constructive as focused response, the presenter selects a focus.
- Students take turns commenting on the work. They begin by referencing something that was done well. They may ask for clarification. They can offer a suggestion. Group members listen to one another and avoid repeating what the other students have already said.
- The presenting student listens without comment. She may make notes. When everyone is done, she decides her next steps. She may elect to follow the suggestions of her classmates or to remain with her original work. The author always owns the work.
- The next student in the group presents his work and the process is repeated.

You can use the same process, with some revision, in a math class, for example. The presenting student selects a problem he had wrong. He shows the group the steps he took to get the answer. The group assists the presenting student in understanding where he went wrong, and offers instruction for redoing the problem. This takes time, but since the best way to retain information is to teach it to someone else, it's time well spent.

For group feedback to be most effective, students should leave with an individual plan for their next steps. A great benefit of small groups assisting one another as they improve their work is that while students are working in groups they are all engaged. They have the full attention of their peers; they don't have to wait for the teacher's feedback. When groups are working well it is tempting to stay behind your desk and do paper work. Instead, walk around the room, listen in, add a comment when appropriate, redirect a question a student asks you to another student. The more you nurture and respect their ability to help one another, the more "teachers" there will be in the classroom, and the fewer papers you'll take home.

When you learn to let go, to recognize that the teacher's perspective is not the only one, you'll learn from your students, and they will learn from one another. They'll make comments and offer suggestions you hadn't thought of yourself. If they do advise someone incorrectly, you can catch it later, or the students will. Remember, this is group work, and if you've provided the instruction in advance, the probability is high that one or more of the group members will be on target or will ask you for clarification.

Grading

Although putting a grade on student work is a form of feedback, grades constitute terminal feedback. Once you assign a grade, students are done with the work, even if the grade is a Fail. When I have decided to grade student work, A, B, or C work receives a grade. There is no D in my classes because we are standards-based and D doesn't meet the standards. (See Chapter Six, "Student Portfolios," and Chapter Four, "Beginning with the End in Mind.") I mark poor-quality work, "Not yet ready for a grade," and add two prescriptive comments for improvement.

If student portfolios are part of your practice (I sincerely hope they are), and students regularly reflect on their work, make revision and redemption a possibility. Allow students to revise their work and resubmit it. They are more likely to revise work if it has not yet received a grade. If the goal is for all students to achieve x, then allow time for students to examine past work and to revise it.

What happens if all the work is not graded? What would it look like if you graded some work and only commented on other work? Before answering, let's revisit why we grade work in the first place.

Sorting

What are the consequences for students when we predetermine a bell-shaped distribution of grades? The few at the A end feel great; those at the opposite end don't. With a bell-curve, if the assessment was particularly difficult, or poorly constructed, and no one did well, some students still get an A. Conversely, if the assessment was very easy, everyone might do very well, but still only a few would receive an A. Sorting is about someone winning and someone else losing. But learning shouldn't be competitive. When students compete for grades, they are reluctant to help one another, don't offer constructive criticism, and aren't as cooperative—is that the type of classroom community you want to create? Everyone can and should learn. If you're using a standards-based approach, then a student's grade is dependent on demonstrating individual accomplishment. If the assessment is aligned to the standards, and you measure student work against a preestablished rubric, then grades are *more* objective (there is no *truly* objective grading). With modeling and practice, students can grade themselves against the rubric and monitor themselves as they progress toward achieving the standard. Each student can demonstrate their learning. There is no finger pointing as in, "If Adrienne weren't in the class, I'd have the top grade," or "At least I did better than Adrienne did."

Gauging Student Progress

Students and parents want to gauge student progress. Great, they should be aware of the progress that is being made toward meeting or surpassing the goals. I don't believe there's a better or easier way to study student's progress than with a student-led conference. (See Chapter Eight.) Students identify their learning goals (the standards or others), present to their parents or other significant adults their evidence in the form of the work they have done or are in the process of doing, and then discuss what they've learned, what they are struggling with, what their next steps are, and how all of the significant parties can work together. There is no ambiguity about how the student is progressing because the evidence is visible.

When the teacher is the sole source of grading, students don't have to own their grades. It's easier to blame poor grades on a teacher "who doesn't like me" than on a lack of effort or poor study habits. This is especially true of lower-performing students. Instead, students can learn how to assess their own learning and assign their own grades. This takes modeling with examples and rubrics to measure against. Of course, teachers maintain the final say, but over time, students learn to assess themselves fairly accurately. Learning to self-assess accurately is more important than having an outsider, the teacher, always determine the grade. Monitoring your own productivity means adjusting the amount and quality of your own output without being instructed to do so by others. It is about being a self-starter.

Required Grades

Colleges require grades. Course grades should be based on *clear, consistent, and convincing* evidence of student achievement. The course grade should represent a total body of work, done over time, not a single snapshot or final exam. Therefore, you don't have to grade every piece that goes into the portfolio: the body of work, teacher-graded or student assessed, will speak for itself. If you only have four grade options, A, B, C, and F, it becomes very easy to agree on the final grade. If you're using numerical grading (1–100 percent), there's more flexibility, but the grade family remains easy to determine.

District Mandates

The school district makes us grade, it's true. In every district I've worked, and in all those I've studied, the district requires grades. But it doesn't tell you what to grade or how to grade. A grade can be a check mark for completing homework, or a numerical entry representing quantity, or a full-blown grade, or double grade for an extensive project, or just about anything else you decide to measure.

Self-Reported Grades

I use the honor system for recording homework grades. It works well, it teaches the students about personal responsibility, and it takes very little time. When I assign homework—a draft or revision, some reading or preparation of questions for future discussion, or any other assignment where the benefit is in doing the homework itself, I ask students to put their homework on their desks on the due date. I ask students who don't have their homework to put a blank sheet of paper on their desks. I can see their work, or what appears to be their work, as I quickly walk about the room, or peer from the podium where I stand with the roll book. Homework assignments are usually worth ten points (although I never add the points; they just represent a percentage of the possible total, an indication of what the student did). When I call a student's name, they respond with how many points they have earned. Ten points means you put in a lot of effort and really applied yourself. Two points means you intended to work, you put your name and date on the page, you read the assignment, but you didn't do much more. A seven might indicate that you did most of the work, but watched TV at the same time and didn't really apply your whole mind. A blank paper earns zero. I'm not very concerned with absolute accuracy in the grade. What is important is completing the homework so we can build on it. It's also about reporting out, about students' personal responsibility and self-assessment. I can record grades for the entire class in under two minutes, and students are affected by their peers' opinion of them.

Students are warned in advance about honesty, about the embarrassment associated with getting caught inflating a grade. Because students are reporting the points they earned, they are accountable. They own up to what they've done or chosen not to do. If they are embarrassed because they didn't do any work and have to report a zero, they can change their behavior and not be embarrassed the next time. During the balance of the class period students usually work with their homework, continue writing, reading, and discussing. They are engaged in learning activities that are dependent on their having done the homework—why else would you assign it? I circulate and very rarely catch a student who said they had earned an eight but in reality deserved a two. When that does happen, I correct the grade in my roll book, but not without confronting the student in a nonbelligerent manner. Sometimes I only have to ask, "I don't think this is an eight, would you like to revise your points?" Students sheepishly revise their grades and remember their embarrassment the next time they report. It's about owning your work and your behavior.

Read-Arounds

Not all assignments lend themselves to point reporting. There is student work that should be read and commented on and, yes, even graded by the teacher, but not all of the commenting and grading needs to be done by you. Read-arounds are an excellent opportunity for students to evaluate their own work by studying other students' work.

For this strategy, students are in groups of four. Each group is assigned a letter, or number, or animal name (depending upon my mood, current events, or whim), which students write on the top of their work (essays, lab reports, research papers, word problems, etc.). I collect group A's work and pass it to group B. Group B's work goes to group C, and so on. I use a stopwatch for this one. Withing their group, students pick up a paper and read it in one minute (they usually start slowly, but when they realize how much they need to complete in one minute their reading speed picks up) and, when I say, "Change," students pass the paper they've just read or studied to the next person in the group. When all the papers have been studied by each member in the group the students either agree on a grade (if that's the instruction for the day) or they select the best paper of the batch—the one that most closely meets the criteria. We continue to move the papers around until every group has studied every paper. (When I work with a math class, it's generally sufficient to have only two groups read the problems. I make other adjustments for other subjects.) Finally, I ask the groups to identify the work they've selected as best and I read them to the whole class. We discuss the qualities that make it a "best" paper (project, lab report, word problem, etc.). What else might it benefit from?

After reading all the students' papers and hearing the discussion around "best" work, students have the option of submitting their own work that period or of taking it back and revising it. As a result of the read-around students have many models to consider and dozens of responses to the same assignment from which to draw. Students relate more to examples from their peers than to any found in a textbook, or even from a prior class. Even students who have not done the assignment gain a clearer understanding of what to do. There's no time during a one-minute read to copy another student's work.

Here's what generally happens. About 80 percent of the class elects to take their work home for revision while the other 20 percent turn in their work as is. On the next due date about half of the original 80 percent resubmit the same work they were planning to revise but never got around to. The remaining 40 percent have revised their work and usually improved it significantly. Generally, the students who continually revise their work grow academically at an amazing rate throughout the course. Everyone, however, has the option—that's what life is about. Many have the opportunity; those who elect to put in the effort gain the rewards.

In all of the strategies I use with students, even my adult students, it's about ownership, effort, and choice. I provide multiple opportunities for students to demonstrate accomplishment or to choose not to bother. The collective papers I finally read and grade are always much better than their first offerings. There are no losers, there's no competition, everyone can improve.

I'm reading *Pour Your Heart into It* by Howard Schultz, chairman and CEO of Starbuck's. He writes about not taking no for an answer and persevering: "What would have happened had I just accepted his decision? Most people, when turned down for a job, just go away." Similarly, most students when given a grade accept it as final. "So many times," he continues, "I've been told it can't be done. Again and again, I've had to use every ounce of perseverance and persuasion I can summon to make things happen." And then Schultz offers some advice: "Life is a series of near misses. But a lot of what we ascribe to luck is not luck at all. It's seizing the day and accepting responsibility for your future" (1997, 44). That's the lesson I want my students to learn. Success is not about luck; it's about sweat equity. But if we don't provide opportunities for continual improvement, if all our assessments are summative, then students won't attain high accomplishment and they won't develop the skill set necessary for perseverance.

Teacher Grading

When it's the best strategy, I do grade students' work. I plan in advance and collect only the work I know I can grade and return within two days. I don't want to stockpile hundreds of papers until I'm paralyzed by the sheer volume.

I determine in advance what part or parts of the student work I will study and grade in depth and what part or parts I will read lightly, and I stick to it. While grading the class set I keep a computer document open, or a transparency, and write down problems that repeat from one student to the next. These repeating problems or misconceptions often become the subject for a minilesson the next day. Instead of making the corrections on one paper at a time, we work together as a whole class. We correct the work together on the overhead or LCD projected screen, then students correct their papers, sometimes working individually, sometimes with partners. I get the same results, more corrected student work, in a lot less time.

The more accountable talk around academic tasks, the higher the achievement. Students love to correct examples from their own work. Although I don't identify whose paper I took the error or errors from, the students usually identify themselves. When the classroom environment is safe, there's no shame in trying and failing, provided that you stand up and try again. I have been incorporating more and more student-to-student talk around specific tasks, like editing, brainstorming, and grading, and have seen consistent growth.

Reflecting on Learning

A teaching cycle isn't complete until we've reflected on the experience—that's how we all learn. Asking students to reflect on their own work periodically—through their portfolio collections, after completing single assignments, and even while they work—honors learning.

Students who learn about their learning are more likely to be lifelong learners.

Pause and Reflect

There's a lot to consider in this chapter. Assessment is seldom taught during professional development, when we focus mostly on curriculum and instructional strategies. But assessment actually drives learning, or should. Take time to think about the role assessment plays in your teaching and in your students' learning. What are you collecting and grading? What do you need to collect and grade? Other than grading, how else can you provide formative and summative feedback? What would it look like in your practice if you allowed time for revision and redemption?

Chapter Six

Student Portfolios
Collect, Select, Reflect

An educational portfolio is a very personal collection
of artifacts and reflections about one's accomplishments, learning, strengths and areas to strengthen.
The collection is dynamic, ever-growing and ever-
changing. It shows a student's growth (developmen-
tal portfolio), best works (showcase portfolio), or
total output (comprehensive portfolio). It is a tool
for reflection . . . If there is no reflection from the
owner on the materials collected, the collection is
merely a group of artifacts without form and purpose, making it nothing more than a scrapbook.

■R. L. Wyatt III and S. Looper, *So You Have to Have a Portfolio*

The student portfolio is the centerpiece of my teaching, a vehicle for
seamless, invisible classroom management. Throughout the course students *collect* their work, *select* pieces that best represent their progress
and accomplishment, *reflect* on their learning, *assess* what they need to
learn, *revise* as new learning occurs, and *present* to an audience. What
begins as a simple manila folder (or electronic disc or three-ring
binder) has the power to transform a classroom from teacher- and
teaching-centered to student- and learning-centered. Portfolios also
shift the workload from the teacher to the student—where it rightfully
belongs.

Basic Philosophy

Photographers wouldn't dream of going to a job interview without a
portfolio of their best photographs—a collection demonstrating the
range of their photographic accomplishments. Architects have portfolio collections of their renderings. Musicians showcase sheet music and
recordings. Writers have their book and article abstracts. Academicians

have their curricula vitae. In each case, the portfolio collection is evidence of the bearer's accomplishments.

Similarly, student portfolios showcase evidence of students' academic accomplishments. Their advantages are many:

- Portfolios are not competitive. They are about academic growth and are evidence of each student's learning.
- Portfolios are repositories to collect student work.
- Students maintain their own portfolios—they select the work to place in their portfolios, and when appropriate, they take work out.
- Teachers can require certain work be included, or negotiate whenever appropriate.
- Students reflect on the work they've collected. They study their progress toward mastering the targeted instructional goals.
- Students can revise work collected in their portfolios and may redeem their grades with the teacher's approval.
- Students showcase their work during student-led conferences with parents and others.

The Nuts and Bolts

A student portfolio is a simple manila folder. (Although there is some movement toward electronic portfolios, most schools still use manila folders.) Portfolios, one per student, are kept in the classroom. The most common portfolio-management system includes a plastic crate (one per class) and hanging files in which to place the portfolios. That's it. No other special equipment is needed. The initial cost for a class set of portfolios, including the one-time purchase of the plastic crate and hanging folders, is under $10.00. The crates sit in the classroom readily accessible to students.

The Manila Folder

Begin by handing each student an empty manila folder, the plain vanilla variety or colored—it's your preference and your budget. Colored folders are about three times the price of the plain wrap variety. Instruct students to carefully write their full name on the tab— because *they* will have to find the folder each time they use it. Advise them also that they may decorate the folder in any way they choose, but alert them that their parents will be viewing the folders periodically and they should not put any marks on the folder they wouldn't want their parents and others to see. That generally takes care of any thoughts of graffiti. Ownership begins with students' writing their own name.

For the left side of the manila folder I provide handouts that students attach using staplers that I circulate around the room. Passing the stapler(s) around works well, the task can be completed in a few minutes, and it beats your stapling all the handouts to the inside of the students' folders. One handout lists the instructional goals. The terms *instructional goals*, *standards*, and *learning goals* are used interchangeably. You may also include *behavioral goals* (see also Chapter Seven, "Habits of Mind") and a portfolio grading rubric. Because we are talking about learning, and not about points earned, the I've provided an example that focuses on student learning. Grades are earned when students achieve the standards.

The Course Goals

Take a look at the sample handout in Figure 6–1. These standards were compiled from the California Standards for English Language Arts by a group of teachers who studied them, reduced them to a total of nine (only three are shown), and rewrote them in student-friendly language. It is very important that the learning goals be delineated at the beginning of the semester, that there not be too many of them, and that they be written in a language that is accessible to students and to

FIGURE 6–1
Course Goals

Ninth-Grade English Language Arts (Partial)

All students are expected to provide clear, consistent, and convincing evidence of having achieved each of the following standards (substitute instructional and/or behavior goals if you prefer) in order to satisfactorily complete English Language Arts 9A and 9B.

Mastery Level—Grade A
Above Proficient Level—Grade B
Proficient Level—Grade C
Below Basic Level—Grade F

The Standards (instructional goals)

1. Consistently and properly use the conventions of standard written and spoken English.
2. Read 1.25 million words per year (fifteen minutes per day, average).
3. Research, synthesize, and convey information from cited multiple sources.

---

their families. Additionally, teachers should be prepared to explain the importance, beyond the academic environment, of each of the learning goals (standards) to students.

I strongly recommend that you eliminate the "D" grade designation. If you are a standards-based school system, then students either meet the standards or they don't. Teachers frequently report that eliminating the D grades also reduces disruptive behavior because more students are working toward mastery. In middle school and high school D grades are generally considered courtesy grades. Teachers assign them to students who are not so awful that they want to punish them with F grades, but really haven't done much during the semester. The message a D grade sends to the student is actually one that suggests that it is okay to do almost nothing, you'll still get by. I always ask teachers how they feel when the students entering their class for the consecutive course have only attained D grades previously.

Some students work the system. They think their grades don't count, especially in middle school, so they do as little as possible to just get by. This is especially true for those students who don't anticipate going to college. When these same students arrive in high school, where teachers are more prone to assign an F grade to students who don't do their work, the kids are shocked. Dropout rates increase because ninth-grade students realize for the first time that they may not graduate. Grades should reflect learning, not seat time. If you expect little from students, that's what you'll get. Teachers who expect more, and teach accordingly, get more.

One of the urban high schools where I consult has eliminated D grades in English language arts, social studies, and science. Teachers report that some students are initially surprised, but they quickly get over it. Most also pull their grades up to C level. No teachers are reporting more total failing grades than before. Teachers in other departments are also considering dropping the D grades. Consider this: if you are standards-based, then what do D grades say about students' level of accomplishment?

Below basic level can also be interpreted, and stated, as *Failure to accomplish the standards or to meet the instructional goals*. When students see a grade, any grade—even an F, they consider the work complete. If you instead assign *has not yet met the standard*, that sends the message that students are expected to continue their learning; we are not just going to forget it and move on.

Clear, Consistent, and Convincing

Including the words *clear*, *consistent*, and *convincing* at the outset will save you lots of grief later on. *Clear* means that any reasonable person, examining the student work, will find the evidence that the student has achieved the standard. Students can't argue, "Well, if you look between the lines," or "I meant to say," etc. *Consistent* means that throughout the course—not just the week before, or in spurts, but on a regular basis—work is completed, revised, and resubmitted as needed. *Convincing*, although similar to *clear*, has the additional meaning that there has to be ample proof of achievement. Solving one math problem or submitting one error-free paragraph, while evidence, is not sufficiently convincing.

Portfolios are not just collections of quantity, they are also about quality. When explaining the portfolio to students I always use examples from the business workplace. David Thornburg (2002), writing in *The New Basics: Education and the Future of Work in the Telematic Age*, highlights High Productivity—the ability to create relevant, high-quality products—as one of the most important workplace requirements in the twenty-first century. It's not enough for employees to work diligently on payday, they have to produce high-quality work all week long. And the same is true for students.

In another very interesting study, researchers found that only 20.9 percent of students with a high school GPA of C or lower had attained any degree (AA or higher) (Rosenbaum 2001)—and that's more than eight years after high school graduation! How well students do in high school, and especially the habits they develop, affects their income for the rest of their lives—whether or not they attend college. Let's not lie to our students by assigning inflated grades that do not reflect their learning. Nor should we lie to them by assigning grade points for activities not related to the instructional goals. (I passed high school chemistry not by mastering the curriculum, but by doing extra credit posters every week.) I am not suggesting that noncognitive behavior doesn't count. It counts a great deal. Rates of absenteeism, the ability to get along with others, and personal responsibility all affect grades, and later affect success in the workplace, because they affect students' academic work.

The portfolio collection with its accompanying reflective pieces shows the quantity of students' work as well as the quality of their reading, writing, and thinking. If it is accurate that students acquire only 2 percent of the knowledge they will need in their lifetimes in their secondary schooling, then we must pay attention to the quality of student thinking and provide multiple opportunities to develop critical deep-thinking skills (Barth 2001). Portfolios aid this process.

Evidence

In addition to instructional goals, I also provide a list of possible artifacts students may use to demonstrate mastery. The list in Figure 6–2 addresses two of the standards provided as examples in Figure 6–1 and gives examples of assessment forms. Consider other ways for students to demonstrate mastery of these standards. Your assignments should address

FIGURE 6–2
Evidence
of Mastery List

Evidence

Standard 1: Consistently and properly use the conventions of Standard written and spoken English.

- All final copies of written documents included in the portfolio must demonstrate consistent use of Standard written English.
- Prepared oral presentations must demonstrate consistent and proper use of Standard spoken English suitable for the academic setting.

Standard 2: Read 1.25 million words per year.

- reading logs
- book talks
- written or oral discussions around main ideas or other text-related topics
- accelerated reader test results
- essays
- book reports
- reflective reading journal entries
- graphic organizers
- reading journals
- artwork in response to print texts
- annotated book cards
- other, as negotiated between teacher and student

Assessments

- quizzes
- tests
- essays
- original problems with solutions
- homework
- preparing and delivering a lesson teaching a skill
- group projects

Student Portfolios

the targeted standards and provide multiple opportunities to demonstrate their mastery. An artifact may be used for more than one standard.

Differentiated instruction naturally arises when assessments are more open-ended and allow for student choice. Try to include some performance assessments that have elements of reading, writing, speaking, and listening.

Label those items that are mandatory (everyone has to include them) and those that allow for some student choice. I frequently have students begin several essays, even take them through two drafts, but ask them to complete only one or two of their choice.

The *Consortium on Chicago School Research* looked at student work on a large scale to determine the level of intellectual demands placed on elementary-grade students. Although at the primary grades the curriculum was grade appropriate, the work they were assigned became further and further below grade level as the students progressed. By high school, students were frequently assigned upper-elementary work to complete. It's no wonder that students are disengaged. When the work is not challenging, it is not interesting.

Verify your curriculum and assignments against your state standards by grade level. That becomes the targeted goal. Students may arrive in varying stages of readiness for that level of work, but the goal remains the same for all of them. Some will need more time and more scaffolding from you. Some will also need to exert a great deal more effort than they have in the past, a fact many of your students will acknowledge when you bring that discussion forward. Student success is linked to a rigorous curriculum.

Behavioral Goals

Our middle and high school students are in their formative years, when most of their habits develop unconsciously, often as reactions to external influences such as peers, the media, or the perceived "cool" thing to do. In addition to assisting with mastering the curriculum, we can be instrumental in helping students proactively develop positive behaviors, even break negative behaviors, which hinder learning. And we don't have to be behavioral psychologists to do so, just thoughtful teachers who care about the whole child.

Thinking about what I want students to know and be able to do five, ten, or even thirty years from now has increased my awareness of the importance of setting behavioral goals. I examined Thornburg's list of twenty-first-century skills and then adapted the skills to classroom behaviors:

- Inventive thinking and adaptability = engagement and listening;
- Interpersonal skills and social responsibility = classroom interactions;
- High productivity = preparation and attendance.

Behavioral goals support learning and are included in the student portfolio from the outset of the semester or course. When portfolios are reviewed, students reflect on their academic and behavioral goals. They are part of the student-led conference discussion. (Remember, students can attach the behavioral goals handout to their own manila folders—you do not have to do it for them.)

Develop a rubric, or use the example in Figure 6–3 on page 72 as a measurement for behavior goals.

I use the behavior rubric during the first student-led conference. It's a very effective tool that helps students equate their behavior to their academic success, or lack of success. But, as with instructional goals, they need to know the objective in advance so they know what is expected and what goals to work toward. It's about *beginning with the end in mind*.

Reflection: The Key to Meaningful and Productive Student Portfolios

Devoid of the reflective process, portfolios are just scrapbooks, another repository for student work, not much different from the bottom of a backpack, only neater. But when the reflective process is an integral part of the student portfolio, it becomes a dynamic vehicle supporting high-quality learning. Most important, it converts class assignments from something students do to satisfy the teacher and receive a grade into a tool for learning about one's own learning.

Students, like the rest of us, must have some time set aside in the school day to stop producing and start reflecting on what they've already done. This is time spent analyzing their progress toward mastering instructional and behavioral goals. It is also time to establish personal goals for how they will continue toward mastery and beyond.

The First Reflection: Stop and Think

During the first weeks of the course while you and your students are establishing the class norms, building classroom community, identifying

Behavior Rubric

Behavior	Always	Often	Sometimes	Seldom
I attend regularly and am on time for class.				
I bring all materials, including textbooks as required.				
I complete in-class and homework assignments in a timely manner.				
I contribute by offering ideas and asking questions.				
I listen to others and build on their ideas.				
I support the learning community through positive, nondisruptive behaviors.				

FIGURE 6–3 Behavior Rubric

the instructional goals, and tackling the curriculum, instruct students to put their work into their folder for examination at a later time. For students who have never used a portfolio, explain that it's a collection and that they will learn more as time goes on. Students who have used portfolios before are usually interested and often eager to use them again.

We generally do our first portfolio reflection about four weeks into the course, after we've accumulated some assignments and established trust. Portfolio reflection days are wonderful opportunities for you as well, a time to look at what you've been teaching and analyze how effective your teaching has been: It is also a time for you to look at your goals and decide whether to reestablish them or to enlarge, alter, or delete them. It's critically important during this first reflection to take the time to explain to students how they will benefit from reflecting on their work. Then allow them sufficient opportunity to think about the work they have done and the behaviors they have exhibited, and allow additional time to set new goals.

Portfolios, and the reflections that accompany them, are highly idiosyncratic. They reflect what you are doing in class and what you value. The example in Figure 6–4 on pages 74–75 is taken from my ninth-grade English language arts class and reflects what we were doing at the time. Note how the reflections become more complex as the semester continues.

Modeling

Most of your students will not have completed a reflective piece like this one prior to your class. It is imperative that you model a response before expecting students to complete the reflection, otherwise you'll get blank stares and one-line responses. I keep some portfolios from prior semesters to use as examples, or I may ask a student to permit me to use his portfolio and respond as if I were the student. I do a think-aloud as if I were a student in the class while writing on an overhead or onto a computer screen with an LCD projector or TV attachment.

A modeled response to Reflection 4 in Figure 6–4 might read like this:

> I chose to revise my story about the street where I live. When I did the assignment the first time I copied a lot from *House on Mango Street,* but that's not really what my street looks like. In the revised short narrative, I'm more honest. I give more details about what you might see on my street and also add some comments about

Student Four-Week Reflection

Name: _____   Date: _____

- Agendas (total number of agendas attached):   _____
- Vocabulary (total number attached):   _____
- Reading log (total number of entries attached):   _____

Number of days attending class   _____

Number of days tardy or absent   _____

Instructions: For this reflection we will focus on the first two instructional standards. Review all of the work you have done during the first four weeks of this course.

1. Using evidence in your portfolio, in a minimum of one well-written paragraph on a separate sheet of paper, explain the progress you have made toward mastering standard 1 (Consistently and properly use the conventions of standard and spoken English). Refer to specific assignments included in this portfolio. Measure your progress toward Mastery, Above Proficiency, Proficiency, or Below Basic at this time. State specific steps you will take toward attaining mastery of this standard.

2. For standard 2, refer to your reading logs. In a well-written paragraph discuss what you are currently reading outside of assigned reading, why you made this selection, and what you are enjoying reading most (or not enjoying) and why. Use your reading logs to support your commentary.

3. In a separate paragraph, discuss how your attendance and promptness have affected your academic progress so far this semester. Explain the steps you will take to support your positive behavior or change behaviors that do not support your academic progress.

4. Select one piece of work from your portfolio. This can be a graded or ungraded assignment. Revise or complete the piece and include it in the portfolio attached to the top of your earlier work. Explain in a separate paragraph why you chose this piece for revision, what growth you have demonstrated since you originally began or completed this piece, and what you would like me to focus on as I reexamine your work. Finally, if you were assigning a grade for this work, what would it be and why? Refer to the rubric.

FIGURE 6–4 Reflection

5. Using the behavior rubric, assign yourself a grade in work habits (Circle one: E, S, U) and explain below why you have earned that grade.

6. Using the behavior rubric, assign yourself a grade in cooperation (Circle one: E, S, U) and explain below why you have earned that grade.

7. Consider all of the above, and all of what you have accomplished in this class during the first four weeks and assign yourself a grade (Circle one: A, B, C, or F). Explain why this is the grade you have EARNED and which you can support with EVIDENCE included in your portfolio.

8. Optional: Additional comments about anything.

*Students copy agendas daily; they are responsible for adding ten vocabulary words from their reading each week; we read daily either in class or outside of class, and students maintain reading logs. Only work attached to the reflection, or otherwise included in the portfolio, is considered evidence. I don't reward missing work. I don't count or check all of the work, but I spot-check often enough that students tend to report accurately.

FIGURE 6–4 Reflection (continued)

how the street feels. The revised piece is more about me and how I see and feel when I'm on the street. The first time I thought I had to do what you want, just copy and change a few words. Now I know you want us to be real writers, honest ones. I'd like you to focus on what feeling you get when you read about my street.

A response to Reflection 7, the quarterly grade, might read like this:

I deserve a B+ because I always come to class and never make any trouble for you. I know I don't do my work all the time so there's not much in the portfolio but I will.

Comments About the First Reflection

Thinking about your thinking and learning is a high-level activity, one that is not practiced regularly. Expect that the initial reflections will be simplistic. Students who are not doing very well often report inflated grades (as in the sample response to number 7 above) and may miss the whole point about using evidence. Don't despair. By the second reflection five or so weeks later, they really begin to get it.

When there is an inflated grade, as in the example above, I'll respond with: "I looked for evidence to support your B grade, but couldn't find it. Based on the evidence in this portfolio I think you earned an F grade for the first marking period. However, if I am wrong, please provide the evidence and I will change your grade." Generally, that does it and the student understands, is more thoughtful, and actually does more of the work the second time around.

The feedback you provide for your students is critically important. As a high school teacher I've sometimes given sarcastic responses, something along the lines of "You've got to be kidding!" But the reality is that the student with the inflated grade is not kidding. The grade they assign themselves is based on what they've received in the past. Sarcasm is hateful, there's no place for it in the classroom, and it doesn't help to move the student to the desired goal. Students listen to all we say and do—so be mindful.

Sometimes students underreport their efforts and I'll respond, "You indicated you earned a C grade, but based on the evidence I think you should have indicated an A or A- grade. However, I will leave the grade you chose this time. If you would like to reconsider, please do so and put it in writing." My goal is for students to accurately analyze and evaluate their own work—that's an important skill they will need all of their lives. If the grading period is one that goes on the permanent record, I will record the grade earned. I don't want to jeopardize the student's academic standing.

Students who are doing well frequently underreport their efforts while marginal students tend to overreport. This phenomenon interested me when I first identified the pattern in my students' responses. I had read previously that competent people continually question their own competency, never thinking they are doing well enough. On the other hand, incompetent people rarely question themselves because they are too incompetent to know they are not competent. Students' reactions to grading themselves were much the same. Consider the following:

> Studies of students' causal attributions—their explanations for success or failure—show that successful students tend to attribute their success to internal factors, such as effort (which they can control) and ability (which is beyond their control), and their failures to external factors, such as bad luck, a difficult test question, or a teacher's grading error. Their conviction that effort brings about success leads them to exert more effort when they encounter a learning challenge. Unsuccessful students, on the other hand, tend to attribute their successes to external factors, such as an easy exam or good luck, and blame their failures on internal factors not under their control, such as their lack of ability. These attributions lead unsuccessful students to conclude that they can do little to increase their level of achievement. (Kozminsky and Kozminsky 2003)

It's very important that students understand the cause and effect of their own behavior if we ever hope to assist our underachieving students. If you believe that what you do does not impact the outcome, then there is no reason for you to attempt any different behavior; the existing behaviors are good enough.

Although I know this to be true, I'm continually surprised when I see how seldom underachieving students make the connection between effort and results. While mentoring a math teacher I asked his students to do a reflection based on their week's work. Students wrote down the number of days they attended class (attendance was extremely poor in this class), and the number of homework assignments they had completed. We then computed the percentages based on the number of days class had been in session and the number of homeworks assigned. Figuring the percentages, especially when they saw 20 or 30 percent, was already eye-opening. We then returned their graded unit test papers and asked them to compare the percentage of their attendance and completed homework to their test scores. The teacher and I weren't surprised that the correlation between them was high, but the students were.

Students in this algebra class, however, where most were repeating, had not made the connection that practice in math, as in doing one's homework, impacted their learning. They saw homework and tests as two unrelated events. Students who come from academically rich homes come to school with this understanding already built in. But many other students don't. They need to be directly taught that using effective strategies, as taught in school or at home, coupled with their efforts will yield success—whether in school or at work. Reflecting on the evidence in their portfolios bridges the gap in their understanding between cause and effect.

The Value of Reflection

Nurturing students' thinking about their own learning shifts the responsibility for learning from the teacher to the student. Instead of *The teacher didn't teach me*, the conversation becomes *What did I do, or not do, to accomplish this task, to learn this skill?* Reflection takes time. It means teachers have to provide the structure and model the tasks, then allow students to think. There are those of us who are anxious to fill every moment and don't like the quiet that can be interpreted as "doing nothing" time. And students are happy to let us do all the work. I recall the professor from my teacher-education methods class telling us to have a dispatch on the board before the students enter the room, to plan for more than we can possibly finish so we are not surprised by empty time, and then to have a concluding activity. No time to just ponder what we've been doing, what we've learned, or what we want to learn. But it's during these reflective periods that we reinforce our learning and move new learning into long-term knowledge.

The Learning Journal

Instead of adding more information at the end of the class period, consider having students make a daily or weekly entry in a learning journal. I ask my students—children and adults—to explain something they've learned during the class and something we've discussed or studied that they still have questions about, or want to know more about. There are several benefits. First, students know they are accountable for paying attention and for actually learning something. They have to be actively engaged. Second, stating what they have learned reinforces their learning. And third, the following day we can begin with their unanswered questions as we continue the work.

Asking students at the beginning of the period if there is something from the prior day's lesson they didn't get is unlikely to yield positive results. What we have failed to learn, we don't remember and most likely will not be able to ask about. But if we've written down that which we're unsure about, then we can ask for clarification at the next opportunity.

Learning journals can be part of the students' portfolio collection. They may refer to what they've recorded during the semester as further evidence of their learning.

The Second Reflection

The schools where I taught had two twenty-week semesters per school year. English language arts for sixth through eleventh grade is a two-semester course. Because we had four reporting grades each semester, we did portfolio reflections to coincide with the grading periods—eight times each year. While students analyzed and evaluated their progress, I had an opportunity to conduct individual student conferences, do lesson planning, catch up on other paper work, or write in my journal. For the first student reflection and portfolio collection I was the only audience, but for the mid-semester reflection we invited parents to our student-led conferences—that's when student progress really takes a leap. (See Chapter Eight, "Student-Led Conferences.")

The sample ten-week portfolio review in Figure 6–5 on page 80 reflects the work assigned in my ninth-grade English language arts class during one particular semester. No two years were ever alike. Likewise, your portfolio reflections will be unique to your class. In past workshops I have attempted to provide generic portfolio outlines for participants,

English 9—Ten-Week Review
Due: Thursday, November 10. No late portfolios accepted.

Name: _____   Date: _____

Put your portfolio together with the most recent work nearest to the top. Put your letter to me about your work on top of everything else.

1. Agendas since last report card (total number attached):   _____
2. Vocabulary since beginning of semester (total number attached):   _____
3. Reading logs since beginning of semester (total number attached):   _____
4. Grade received on _____ project   _____
5. Journal grade   _____

Instructions: Review all of the work in your portfolio. On a separate piece of paper, write to me using friendly letter format with a paragraph, or more, for each statement in response to each of the following:

1. Discuss the progress (or lack of progress) you are making with your outside reading. When do you do your reading? How often are you reading? What books have you read? What have you enjoyed or not enjoyed and why? What do you plan to read next?

2. Discuss your role (what *you* did) in the drama-mystery group assignment you just completed. If you were the teacher, what grade would you give yourself for group participation on this project and why?

3. Discuss your work habits. When do you do homework? What kinds of assignments help you to learn the most? Explain.

4. Give yourself a solid piece of advice and then discuss why you will or will not follow your own advice.

5. Select two of the standards not addressed in the last portfolio reflection and for *each* describe your progress toward mastery. State the steps you will take to achieve mastery. Refer to the evidence in this portfolio to support your response.

6. Referring to the behavior rubric, what have you learned by listening to other students? Refer to specific events if possible.

7. Consider the evidence and assign yourself a grade in work habits (Circle one: E, S, U) and explain why you earned that grade.

8. Assign yourself a grade in cooperation (Circle one: E, S, U) and explain why you have earned that grade.

9. Finally, consider all of the above and all you have accomplished during the first ten weeks of this semester and assign yourself a grade (Circle one: A, B, C, or F). Explain your grade.

10. Suggestions for what you would like to study during the balance of this semester.

11. Optional: other comments

FIGURE 6–5 Ten-Week Portfolio Review

but they never seem to work. Too generic doesn't satisfy anyone, too specific may not be transferable to someone else's practice. More discussion will follow about how to write your own reflective exercises.

Student-Led Conferences

The ten-week (or mid-semester) reflection (see Figure 6–6) is the basis for the first student-led conference. For a detailed description of these conferences, turn to Chapter Eight, "Student-Led Conferences."

Year-End Student-Led Conferences

The year-end student conference serves an important purpose. During this conference students justify their final grades, the grades they have earned, and their promotion to the next course. Final grades are based on student learning. Prior to the conference students have organized their portfolios (see Figure 6–6 on page 82) and are prepared to demonstrate what they have learned and the grade they have earned. Parents are part of this conversation and decision. In my extensive experience parents rarely wanted their students to be promoted if they had not mastered the course material. The parents are also more likely to hold their students accountable when grades and promotion are directly based on the evidence in the student portfolio. (See Chapter Eight, "Student-Led Conferences," for a detailed explanation of and instructions for conducting the conference.)

Pause and Reflect

What would your professional portfolio look like? What would you select to include and why? How well would your collection demonstrate masterful teaching? Where is there room for improvement? What could you celebrate? What might be the value of maintaining a professional portfolio at the same time your students collect and reflect upon their work? What would be the benefit or challenge to having an audience for your professional portfolio?

End-of-Semester or End-of-Year Reflection

Instructions to students: This is your opportunity to demonstrate what you have learned this semester/year in English 9A/B. Organize the evidence in your portfolio to best demonstrate how you have mastered the standards. You may use the same work to address your accomplishments in more than one standard.

- Begin by dividing your work into evidence piles for each instructional goal, applying multiple labels to any work that crosses over into more than one standard. (Use sticky notes or other means of labeling.)

- For each standard, explain how the evidence included in your portfolio demonstrates a level of Mastery, Above Proficiency, Basic Proficiency, or Below Basic. Remember that you are to provide clear, convincing, and consistent evidence of accomplishment for each standard.

- If there is any work in your portfolio that you have completed or revised after the initial due date and that remains ungraded at this time, explain what you have done and why the work should be reconsidered.

- In a reflective letter, discuss the following:
  - an assignment that demonstrates your ability to think creatively;
  - an assignment that you didn't understand at first but then came to master;
  - an assignment you continue to have questions about;
  - an assignment that you learned from and is important to you;
  - another task of your choice that has special meaning;
  - any additional comments you choose to make about the course, its contents, the classroom environment, the conferences, etc. (Your remarks are important to help me to improve as a teacher; they do not affect your grade either up or down.)

- When you have categorized and evaluated the evidence of learning in your portfolio, explain whether you have demonstrated Mastery (A Grade), Above Proficiency (B Grade), Proficiency (C Grade), or have failed to demonstrate accomplishment (Fail).*

- Review your behavior, including timeliness and completeness of assigned work, and then assign yourself grades for cooperation and work habits. Explain your grades using evidence.*

*Note to reader: The terms *mastery, above proficiency, proficiency,* and *below basic* are taken from the California Department of Education publication *Aiming High* (Norton and Greco 2002).

FIGURE 6–6 End-of-Semester or End-of-Year Reflection

Chapter Seven

Habits of Mind
Behaviors That Make
for Student Success

The illiterate of the twenty-first century will not be those who cannot read and write, but those who cannot learn, unlearn, and relearn.

■*Alvin Toffler*

One of the most important things I do as a teacher is help students form and reinforce effective academic habits. When they have positive academic habits classroom behavior supports learning—another invisible classroom management technique. I first became interested in this work while studying and then teaching Benjamin Franklin's autobiography. In it he describes how he listed behavioral habits he wished to address, then focused attention on his progress in a daily journal. My students use Franklin's method to change their own habits, and so do I.

Students select one thing they wish to change, over which they have control, and then record their progress daily, focusing only on the one identified concern. For instance, a student may want to have a better relationship with her mother (a common concern). While she can't try to directly change her mother's behavior, she can work on how she behaves and reacts to her mother. Every day the students write about what happened, what they do and say. I'm never surprised when, in two weeks' time the student reports that her relationship with her mom has substantially improved.

A habit is something that we do repeatedly. Habits are important, they shape our character. Once students realize they can control their own behavior, and are responsible for the choices they make, they know they can also control their academic behavior. When we are mindful of our behavior, we can change our ways—personal and academic. Students don't have to remain underperforming if they don't want to.

Here's how I hook students: Imagine if every morning you had to rethink about the reasons why you should shower or brush your teeth or even get out of bed. You do it because it's a habit. Not having to think about these actions allows you to think about other things. Habits are learned behaviors, and they can be unlearned. The first way to address a habit is to identify it. What are you doing and why? If it's a habit that you come home from school and turn on the TV, ask what function this serves, what need it fulfills, and what it prevents you from doing. Depending upon your response, you can either decide to keep doing what you're doing, or change it. It takes about two weeks to break a habit or to make one.

What we've been very good at is teaching students to be dependent on teachers. For example, during my education methods classes we were told that when we give an assignment we should thoroughly tell the students what we expect from them—not too much argument there. Then we should tell them again, write it on the overhead or white board or provide a handout, check for understanding, and then tell them one more time. Here's the problem: what we've succeeded in doing is teaching them that they don't have to pay attention until the fourth or fifth repetition. Yet the ability to listen actively is most closely associated with academic success. We do our students a great disservice when we repeat ourselves on a regular basis. College professors don't repeat. Employers don't repeat. Meetings and discussions are not repeated.

In the rush of the school day, in our effort to "cover the curriculum" we seldom stop to allow students to think about what they are learning, how are learning, or even why they are learning. If we want our students to be lifelong learners, then we need to teach that skill and turn the responsibility for learning over to the student. Hence, effective classroom management includes reflective portfolios that include attention to academic habits of mind.

In addition to the academic pursuits and analysis in your student portfolios, consider including some of these Habits of Mind based upon Sean Covey's book, *The 7 Habits of Highly Effective Teens* (Covey 1998).

Here are Covey's seven habits for effective teens, followed by some classroom-based commentary and suggestions:

1. Be Proactive

Take responsibility for your life. For example, doing homework is a decision students make. Did you know that only 14 percent of students who have a C average in high school will eventually graduate from college? Equally important, those who do homework in secondary school earn an average of 13 percent more in their lifetimes than those who don't regularly do their homework. Let's tell students the truth—habits are important and will impact their lives, positively or negatively. Help them to make decisions about what they're going to do and then to plan or take action toward achieving those goals.

How they live their life is largely a choice, their choice, not someone else's. As we have seen, teens who do not do well in school tend to blame outside forces: *My teacher doesn't like me; My mom overslept and didn't get me to school on time; Someone took my textbook out of the locker so I couldn't do the homework.* On the other hand, teens who do well academically identify what they did to be successful: *I do my homework every day as soon as I come home; I don't miss school; I balance my play time with my work time.* Ask your students to identify one thing they can take charge of, and then do it. Turn the responsibility for their learning, and the tools to be successful, over to them.

2. Begin with the End in Mind

Define your mission and goals in life. Of all of the habits worth developing, the one that we can use in our classrooms perhaps most effectively is the habit of goal setting. You can't get there if you don't know where you are going. This is equally true when we establish our goals for the semester, when students know in advance what those semester- or year-long goals are, and when we set personal goals. Help students determine where they want to be academically in your class. If they want to do A work and earn that grade, what do they have to do now in order for it to happen? Success is not an accident. In spite of the game shows and the widely advertised lottery millions, it's rare for success to fall into your lap. Success is the result of planning and hard work. Help students identify a goal and then explicitly state the steps they will need to reach that goal.

3. Put First Things First

Prioritize, and do the most important things first. This is the opposite of the habit of procrastination. Procrastination is a bad habit to fall into. It involves doing those things first that are the easiest, or the most fun—like eating chocolate or watching TV—instead of what is more important at the time—like exercising. The rule for prioritizing applies for talking on the phone with friends or doing one's homework. Get the homework done, then do the other things that are less important in terms of reaching goals you've set for yourself. When we put the last things first, we rarely ever get to the first things. After a couple of hours of TV watching and talking on the phone, who wants to do homework?

4. Think Win-Win

Have an everyone-can-win attitude. Thinking "only one person can get to the top so I'm either going to be the one or I won't even try," is a no-win situation. Teach students to do the best they can and to help others to do their best. Everyone wins in the long run because it's all about relationships, not competition. Help students work together in cooperative settings where there is responsibility built in for one another's success. Cooperative workplace teams accomplishing tasks are becoming more and more common. Let's build on one another's strengths. What are you doing in the classroom to assure equity and equal access to opportunities for success?

5. Seek First to Understand, Then to Be Understood

Listen to people sincerely. Listening has to begin with the teacher. Work on allowing for wait time. As stated before, the average time between a teacher's asking a question and either answering it themselves or asking another question to another student is less than three seconds! Learn to listen and wait. Require students to respond to another student's comments before adding commentary of their own. This is a perfect strategy to employ during Socratic seminars. The skill most closely associated with academic success is *listening*. Listening is not the same as being quiet. Teach students to actively listen to others, to think about what has been said and its implications before responding. Usually we are so full of what we are going to say next that we don't listen at all. When we learn to listen to others, we eventually learn to listen to ourselves. Mindful silence can be good.

6. Synergize

Work together to achieve more. There is an art to working together. Putting students into a group and then assigning a task doesn't guarantee that they will work together to achieve more. The task needs to be clearly defined. The group needs time to work out who will do what, when, and how. We seldom provide enough time for group members to get comfortable with one another. Consider the implications of assigning team members, of allowing students to select their own members and to develop some rules for working together. It takes time to become a group with a common goal. Help the group to set some goals, long term and short term, so the task gets done with a high level of quality.

7. Sharpen the Saw

Renew yourself regularly. Build in time for reflection; it's critical. In our rush to get things done, to cover the curriculum, to fill every minute, we don't stop to renew and refresh. There isn't anything in nature that doesn't take the time for rejuvenation—that's what the dormant winter season is all about. Make time for students to refresh themselves, to take a deep breath, to rethink their habits and goals, to consider their learning and behavior. Time for reflection and portfolio reviews is not time taken from teaching, it's time added to learning.

As you are developing the portfolios for your class, think about what academic habits you might include. It's not just about students' academic achievement. A report from researcher and author James E. Rosenbaum stresses the importance of developing these nonacademic skills. This is worth sharing with your students:

> Employers report that for many jobs, non-academic skills (like timeliness, diligence, and social competence) are key (Shapiro and Iannozzi 1999). Analyses of a national survey indicate that students' educational attainment and earnings nine years after graduating from high school are significantly related to their non-cognitive behaviors in high school—sociability, discipline, leadership, homework time, and attendance—even after controlling for background characteristics and academic achievement.
>
> . . . for some low-achieving high school students, getting a good job after high school can be more lucrative than trying to earn a college degree . . . . only about 14 percent of students with C averages or lower in high school earn a college degree (B.A. or A.A.). Of these low-GPA high school students, those who do complete a B.A. will typically earn 4.3 percent more than students without a college degree—but this is less than one-third the extra earnings that the typical college graduate enjoys. Those

with low high school GPAs who earn an A.A. will typically earn 7.2 percent less than high school graduates with no college degree. (Rosenbaum 2001, 172)

In this time of academic accountability and multiple-choice standardized testing, it's difficult to justify including habits of mind as part of the curriculum, but it pays off. Students who gear themselves to think about goals, to consider their own responsibility for their actions, and to be mindful are also going to pay more attention to their academic life and to the importance of the test scores on their school records. Nothing happens in isolation. Students who consider their work habits, like coming to school, are also more likely to show up on test day and do well.

Pause and Reflect

How do your habits support or impede achieving your personal goals? How do your teaching habits, the curriculum you select, and the strategies you employ, support or impede students' high-level learning? What behavioral changes that you control could significantly impact your students' achievement? What are the next steps toward taking more control over yourself and allowing students to be more responsible for themselves?

Chapter Eight

Student-Led Conferences
Letting Kids Talk

The medium is the message . . . There is a basic principle that distinguishes a hot medium like radio from a cool one like the television, or a hot medium like the movie from a cool one like TV . . . . Hot media are . . . low in participation, and cool media are high in participation or completion by the audience.

■Marshall McLuhan, *Understanding Media*

Student work is the message, and student-led conferences are absolutely cool, requiring high participation and audience involvement. That's why they work so well. When students examine and explain their work before an audience of significant others, usually parents and siblings, everyone is involved.

Forgive me for using a cliché, but it does take a village to educate a child. Secondary teachers, valiantly trying to go it alone, do not have a successful history of engaging parents in their children's education. Generally, phone calls go home when we have problems—when students are misbehaving—or for extracurricular prowess, such as winning an athletic event, but not for academic progress. We can cite many reasons for the lack of contact, but there is no need to spread any blame. A student load of 150 or more is enough reason not to call home for nonemergency issues. Student-led conferences provide an effective way to reach all parents, in a short amount of time, and focus on what parents want to know about—their students' academic progress.

The Guiding Principles

Visualize a room filled with students and the significant adults in their lives. While students present and explain their carefully selected work, adults are thoughtfully engaged with them in an academic conversation around what has been learned, what is still to be learned, and how the student and adults can work together toward the goal of improved student achievement. The teacher, without a roll book, greets students and their guests, and then stands to the side. There are many principles at work here that are key to student success.

- Students present their work to an audience (beyond the teacher).
- Many students present their portfolios at the same time since the teacher acts only as facilitator.
- Teachers do not bring their roll books to these conferences. As soon as the roll book appears parents gravitate toward it to see what the teacher recorded, effectively ending the student-led part of the conference.
- Parents can arrange to meet with the teacher at another time, although they seldom need to. They learn all about their child's progress, or lack of progress, at the student-led conference directly from their student and a joint examination of the student's accumulated work.
- Students engage their audience in a discussion around their learning, their goals for future learning, and the steps they will take to achieve those goals.
- Because the conferences are meaningful to the student and family and relevant to the academic setting, participation is high, significantly higher than for most traditional Back-to-School and Open House events.
- Students sometimes request assistance from the audience, usually parents and family, to meet their goals.
- Conferences are conducted in whatever language is comfortable and familiar to parents and students—no translation required.
- Because of the public setting, students who are not performing well feel safe and are able to discuss their work with their parents without fear of being yelled at, or worse.
- Students and parents who sometimes feel uncomfortable can follow a script (see the sample script below) for their first academic conference.

Whenever possible, plan to hold student-led conferences on the same evening as other teachers. The more teachers participating, the easier the work, the greater the adult turnout, and the higher the level of excitement throughout the school around looking at student work.

Parents are sure to attend when their children have student-led conferences in several subjects on the same evening or weekend day.

The first few times I held student-led conferences, I was the lone teacher at our high school. Later on I teamed up with a science teacher who had many of the same students. Sometimes we added a poetry or choral reading. There were evenings when we played a videotape of student presentations recorded earlier in the week and displayed students' science projects. No matter the setup, student-led conference events are always about students and their learning. When there is dialogue between the student and adult about behavior, and it does sometimes come up when parents are asking why there is not more work in the portfolio, the conversations are always around how the inappropriate behavior doesn't support student learning.

Conference Preparation Begins the First Day of School

I begin preparing students for their student-led conferences on their first day of school. When I distribute the new manila folders that will become their portfolios, I advise them that their parents will be reviewing their portfolios during the year. With the exception of those few students who may have participated in similar conferences in the past, students either don't know what I mean or don't believe their parents will attend. I assure them that their parents will attend and advise them to act accordingly. All the work they do, or don't do, will be part of what they will eventually present to their parents. This is not a threat, just a statement of fact. The initial letter home includes the dates for the upcoming conferences throughout the semester or year. During the next few weeks I make a few casual references to parents viewing what students are putting into their portfolios.

When we do our first reflection, around week four of a twenty-week semester, I ask students whether they would be proud if their parents saw the work they are doing. If they would not be proud, I ask them what changes they will have to make, because we will be having conferences at week ten. A few more students become believers, or have heard by now from former students.

Before week ten we confirm the evening for student-led conferences. The first year I offered conference times once during a weekday evening (this was unpaid time, but well worth it) and for several hours on Saturday. Since then I conduct conferences only one evening each semi-semester, and anytime during a designated teaching day. I arrange for senior students from our service club to provide baby-sitting and I ask parents to provide refreshments. I'm the conductor, not the orchestra.

Invite Them and They Will Come

Students write letters home inviting their parents and/or other significant adults (see Figure 8–1). Student-generated letters, personalized by each student, are much more effective than teacher letters photocopied and distributed. Letters can be supplemented by automatic dialing systems available at many schools. Few handwritten letters end up at the bottom of backpacks.

I generally put some guidelines on the board—date, time, place, reminder about baby-sitting and refreshments, for students to use in writing their own letters. I'll also read one or two letters former students have written. The letter writing is an assignment that frequently makes its way to the student portfolio, further evidence of mastery of the standards. Letters are more or less sophisticated depending on student ability and interest. This assignment is a good example of differentiated instruction. Everyone has the same assignment but they perform based on their personal ability and motivation.

Students have been known to get very creative with their invitations. Thanks to computers, invitations can be in color or can resemble party invitations more than letters, but they must always contain information about why this is an important event. Invitations are an easy-to-grant opportunity for students to be creative, to have choice, and to present the invitation in a way that will elicit the greatest response from their families.

Getting Students and Their Families to Attend

I place a great deal of importance on these conferences. I talk about them frequently. I have photos on the bulletin board taken during past conferences. I assure students who are underachieving that their parents will eventually see the failing grades anyway so it's better to come clean in public. Parents won't yell at their students in front of other parents and students or the teacher. (On only one occasion did a parent slap her son during the conference. She said she worked every day so he could have an education and he repaid her by doing nothing. Wow.

Sample Student-Generated Letter

Date

Dear Parent (Insert name here),

I am very excited to invite you to our first (second) student-led conference of the semester. I promise you an evening to remember where I will be the star. You and I will be looking at and talking about the work I have been doing in English (science, math, social studies/history, world languages, or whatever class or classes apply). This conference is different from any that you have attended in the past (or just like the one we had in fifth grade). Instead of talking to my teacher and checking my grades in the roll book, we'll be studying the portfolio of work that I have done during the past __ weeks.

I know that you are working hard and that it is difficult for you to come to my school, but this is very important to me. I know that my education is important to you and I want you to see what I am doing. We can talk about ways I can do even better and maybe figure out how you can help me. I want you to be proud of me.

In addition to reviewing my work portfolio you will also have a chance to see my group perform in person (or on a video we taped in class). I also have a science project that will be on display. All the families will be bringing some refreshments to share so it will be very nice. Could you bring that spice cake you make better than anyone else in the world? We have free baby-sitting available so you can bring (names of other children). I would also like (older siblings, other family members) to attend.

Please plan to attend on day, time, place: (multipurpose room, classroom, library).

Your loving son/daughter,

RSVP: Complete and return to teacher.
Student Name:
Parent will/will not attend.
Parent will need/will not need baby-sitting services.
Parent will/will not bring refreshments.

FIGURE 8–1 *Sample Student-Generated Letter*

I didn't know what to do, but her son started working more and eventually did graduate.) Students who are doing well want to show off to their parents, and students who are trying, but struggling, welcome the help.

I encourage students to attend even if their parents can't come. For those students who do attend alone, and there are some at every conference, I ask another parent to act as the surrogate. They are happy to assist. Students bring aunts and uncles, older siblings, best friends. Although there's generally about 50 percent participation in our urban settings during the first conference of the semester, by the exit conference in June I have nearly 100 percent attendance every year.

Scripting the First Conference

Students are understandably nervous about the first conference. What will they say to their parents? How will their parents react to their work? To their lack of work? If parents are not educated, will they understand the work the students present? What will happen next? We rehearse in class. Students role-play being alternately the parents and the students. We prepare a script for the first conference and use it in our role playing (see Figure 8–2). At the conference, all participants have a script and are encouraged to follow it.

Post-Conference Reflection

After the conference, students and adults separate so each can write a reflection about their conference experience. Adults may write in their language of comfort.

Instructions to Students
In your reflection on the conference, please indicate what went well and what you might do differently for the next conference. If you have any suggestions on how we can make the conferences more relevant and meaningful, please add your comments. If you would also like to write a letter to your parents, you may do so.

Instructions to Adults
Reflect here on what you learned about your child and how you can assist your child to be more successful in the future. I (the teacher) will

Sample: Student-Led Conference Script

English 9A welcomes you to our first student-led conference. In order that we might all get the most out of the time we have together we are asking each student and parent to follow the script in the order in which it is written.

STUDENT: Thank you for coming to my presentation. Your coming here today was important to me because _____.

ADULT: I am happy to be here because _____.

STUDENT: This semester (quarter/year) my goals are to _____. (Explain your academic goals and your behavior goals including why these goals are important to you.)

ADULT: Thank you for sharing your goals with me. Please show me something that you did this semester (quarter/year) of which you are especially proud.

STUDENT: I am most proud of this work because _____. (Select work and explain why this piece was selected.)

ADULT: (Make a positive comment about the work your student has just shared with you.)

STUDENT: Now I want to show what I am currently working on. (Show and explain your work in progress.)

ADULT: (Comment on the work in progress.)

STUDENT: Let me show you some more of the work I am doing. (Present the rest of the portfolio to the adult.)

ADULT: (Make a positive comment about the collection in the portfolio.) How can I assist you with your school work?

STUDENT: You can help me by _____ . (Make suggestions that are within the scope of possible. For instance, you might suggest more quiet time, or a desk, or turning off the TV, or transportation to the library.)

ADULT: I can help you by _____. (Make a commitment to assisting student's academic progress.)

STUDENT: Thank you for coming to my student-led conference. I am happy that you saw my _____. Please come again.

ADULT: I am very happy that I came. I learned about _____. I will come again.

FIGURE 8–2 Student-Led Conference Script

appreciate any comments you choose to make which will help us to provide the best educational experience for your child. If you would also like to write a letter to your student, you may do so.

Improving Conferences and Portfolios

The parent and student reflections become my guides as I continually improve the student portfolios and the conferences. I have learned through the years about their pleasure in supplying refreshments (I used to buy everything), about how much easier it is when parents are free to use their home language (initially I had translators and insisted on English so I could walk around and listen in), and about being sensitive to child-care issues for younger siblings (everyone is invited—the bigger the audience, the better). I have incorporated many of the parents' suggestions and as a result do less work myself and have more involved parents.

Outcomes of Student-Led Conferences

You cannot overestimate the effects of student-led conferences. For many students and their families, it is their first opportunity to have a discussion around academic progress since their child left elementary school. Because the conversation is based on evidence contained in the student portfolios, students who are not performing cannot hide and students who are doing very well can receive the praise they are due. Evidence tells the truth. Too often underperforming students blame outside influences for their lack of progress: *The teacher lost my paper*, or *She doesn't like me*, or *I was absent when you took me to the dentist/doctor*. The portfolio clearly states the instructional goals. Your classroom routines provide for agendas and makeup work and due dates. There are additional opportunities for revision and redemption. You have provided students with information about free tutoring, after-school services, and other help they can access as needed. The portfolio evidence eliminates the excuses.

Because conferences are held in a public arena—the school cafeteria, a classroom, or other locale—and because the teacher, classmates, and their families are present, the parent focus is on *how do we make the future better* rather than on placing blame. Students have reported that following the student-led conference their parents provided desks so they can have a place to do their school work. They've also reported losing TV and phone privileges. For a very few underperforming students, their behavior and academic performance doesn't change, but for the majority, work improves after the conference. Students are sometimes surprised that their parents care so much—but that never surprises me.

Year-End Conference

The year-end student conference serves an additional purpose. It is during this conference that students discuss their final grades and their promotion to the next course. Final grades are based on student learning (see Figure 8–3 on page 98). Prior to the conference students have organized their portfolios (see Figure 6–6 on page 81) and are prepared to demonstrate what they have learned and the grade they have earned.

Have No Fear

I will admit to some mild anxiety the first time I asked parents to grade their student's work, but I needn't have had any. All parents, with the exception of one in twelve years, are more demanding than teachers are. They want their children to succeed. They don't want to reward them for work they have not done—not at the secondary level. It is easier for a parent to assess what the child has done in school based on the evidence and several opportunities to participate in student-led conferences than to be objective about chores or home behavior. In my experience parents with limited formal education are the severest critics. They know how important it is for their children to have a good education, to work hard, in order to be successful in the future. They don't support phony promotion. Parents are your allies. Given the opportunity to be meaningfully involved, and some guidance in how best to help their children succeed in school, parents will work with you—invite them in.

Additional Parental Involvement

When parents are fully respected partners in the education of their children, we more than double our effectiveness. Some children come to school from homes where they have full academic advantages—

Example: Final Assessment—to Be Completed by Adult

Instructions: Your student has been asked to demonstrate his/her mastery of the ninth-grade Language Arts Standards as a requirement for successfully completing this course. Your student will explain the standards (instructional goals) and provide clear, consistent, and convincing evidence of accomplishment for each one.

Please assess your students' accomplishments in each of the standards according to the following: Mastery, Above Proficiency, Proficiency, and Failure to provide evidence of accomplishment.

Student's Name: _____   Date: _____

Person(s) completing assessment: _____

Relationship to student: _____

Example:

- Read 1.25 million words per year.

Level of Accomplishment (check one): Mastery ___; Above Proficiency ___; Proficiency ___; Failure to provide evidence of accomplishment ___.

- Formulate opinions and support those opinions with evidence.

Level of Accomplishment (check one): Mastery ___; Above Proficiency ___; Proficiency ___; Failure to provide evidence of accomplishment ___.

(Continue for each of the standards.)

When you have completed reviewing all of your student's accomplishments for the semester (year), determine the total grade you believe, based on the evidence, your student has earned. If the student has accomplished the standards, we will recommend the student be promoted to the next grade. If the student has not provided evidence of accomplishing the standards, then the student may attend summer school, intersession, or repeat the course next semester. Thank you for your continued support throughout the year.

Grade Earned:

Comments:

Signature:

_____

FIGURE 8–3 Final Assessment

computers, high-quality conversations, emphasis on academic work ethics, and recognition of the importance of education. Although I've never met a parent who didn't want their child to be successful in school, I've met many who didn't know how to contribute to their child's success. You can turn parents into your partners by instructing them. Suggest that instead of asking, "Did you do your homework?" (Students usually reply, "I didn't have any," or "I did it in school," or "I already did it.") that parents ask, "Show me your homework." When parents ask, "What did you learn in school today?" and when parents contribute what they learned at work, then conversation around learning continues beyond school time.

Caution: Rewards Ahead

Student-led conferences certainly hold students accountable for their academic work, but they also hold the teacher accountable. You must set high, relevant expectations. You must allow multiple opportunities for students to demonstrate achievement. Revision and redemption become expectations. Student portfolios and the accompanying conferences are also a review of your work as a teacher. Teachers who are themselves lifetime learners, who are constantly seeking ways to improve their instruction, and who know that just as their students are not finished products, neither are they, welcome parent input. When a parent approaches a teacher with, "My child learns better when . . ." or "How can I help?" or "My son is doing so much better than he has ever done before, thank you," how can we not want to hold these conferences?

After an especially great teaching year, when each of our conferences became richer, when students' work improved measurably between conferences, we added a poetry night, had a video running of student performances, and opened the high school multipurpose room because we'd outgrown our previous venues. At that last conference parents wanted to know if the next year's teachers would continue with the conferences—they valued them so much. One parent presented me with a beautiful hand-painted plaque, which still hangs on my office wall. It reads, "Mrs. Mack's Classroom." When a second parent gave me a copy of the movie about an inspiring teacher, *Mr. Holland's Opus*, I openly cried at the tribute.

I'll close this section with words from commercial-famous Mikey: *Try it, you'll like it!*

Pause and Reflect

What are the risks and rewards of opening my teaching to parents and other adults through student-led conferences?

Chapter Nine

Teacher's Strategy Toolbox
Designed with the Student and Teacher in Mind

Many studies show that learning is enhanced when students become actively involved in the learning process. Instructional strategies that engage students in the learning process stimulate critical thinking and a greater awareness of other perspectives. Although there are times when lecturing is the most appropriate method for disseminating information, current thinking in . . . teaching and learning suggests that the use of a variety of instructional strategies can positively enhance student learning. Obviously, teaching strategies should be carefully matched to the teaching objectives of a particular lesson.

■George Mason University, Department of Education

Several years ago I had the pleasure of observing a pre-kindergarten class in an inner-city school. The four-year-olds, sitting on a square of carpet, were busily engaged in sorting blocks. The teacher, Steven Hicks, led a discussion on patterns. Students mimicked the patterns Steven produced with the blocks before them, then in pairs they developed their own patterns. When they had gotten the concept of patterns down, an important concept for reading and numeracy, they moved to their desks where they proceeded to reproduce their original patterns on the handles of paper spring baskets. They continually checked their block patterns, matched crayon colors, and completed their baskets.

In a second pre-K classroom, same school, same day, another group of students happily colored the handles of their paper baskets. No patterns to reproduce, just wild coloring—not a bad thing in itself. However, unlike this second teacher, Steven had a strategy in place. He used blocks to teach patterns, which the students then reproduced, which they later applied to putting letters in order to create the patterns on which words depend. The second teacher's students engaged in an activity, making spring baskets to take home, not a strategy to advance them in their academic learning.

All too often, when I observe in our secondary schools, students are engaged in activities—busy work that helps pass the time, but that provides little or no opportunity for learning. These activities include the Friday basketball games in English classes, the word searches for points or prizes, the countless multiple-choice problems that go on for pages when two or three would be sufficient, watching videos in full rather than in carefully selected sections, and many more. Activities fill time and are sometimes engaging, but seldom have rigorous instructional significance. Strategies, on the other hand, are deliberately chosen for their proven effectiveness in assisting students in mastering instructional goals. Every teacher needs a repertoire of effective strategies. Students have a right to instruction that is interactive, engaging, and meaningful, and that goes way beyond a lecture. They have the right not to be bored by a teacher who has a limited set of teaching tools. To maintain engagement, students need a variety of instructional approaches.

This chapter presents several strategies I have found over time to be extremely effective in increasing student achievement and in reducing the teacher workload. Ideally, the discussion surrounding each strategy presented on the following pages will stimulate additional variations and applications. Before implementing any of the strategies, read them through thoroughly and reflect on possible applications in your practice. Having a variety of effective strategies in your teacher's toolbox and knowing when to use them will keep your students engaged. Working collaboratively with your colleagues to implement these and other strategies will increase your expertise.

Epiphany

Many books have impacted my professional work, but few more so than Patrick Finn's *Literacy with an Attitude* (Finn 1999). Based on Brazilian Paulo Friere's work, Finn defines the education many of our students receive, an education designed to provide just enough literacy and knowledge to keep them dependent. He also identifies those strategies most closely associated with a liberating education, an education designed to create independent thinkers. Although not a substitute for studying Finn's work in its entirety, I have listed below some of those strategies most closely associated with domesticating education and those that are essential for a liberating education.

Strive to reduce your reliance on domesticating strategies and increase the use of liberating ones. Liberating strategies make more sense and actually require less teacher time. They shift the responsibility for learning to the student, where it rightfully belongs.

Domesticating Education = Dependence

Overuse of the following strategies is frequently associated with domesticating education; they do not lead to deep student engagement, critical thinking, or lifelong learning.

- Knowledge is presented as facts isolated from wider bodies of knowledge.
- Teachers don't explain how lessons and assignments are related to one another.
- Knowledge taught is not related to the lives and experiences of the students.
- The work is easy, the expectations low, the belief that students can achieve more are not evident.
- Questioning is primarily level 1—correct answers found in the text.
- Classroom discourse is limited to teacher-student and student-teacher; there is seldom verbal academic exchange between students.
- Students are expected to be compliant; challenges to the text's accuracy or the teacher's authority are put down.
- Instruction is typically copying notes and writing answers to factual questions.
- Work is evaluated on quantity more than on quality.
- Writing is limited to short pieces, filling in the blanks, and completing worksheets.
- Artwork is substituted for written expression.
- The teacher asserts tight control over students and materials.
- A "quiet" classroom is most prized; obedience is highly valued.
- Students primarily work alone.

Liberating Education = Independence

Wide use of the strategies that follow is frequently associated with masterful instruction, which pushes students to take greater responsibility for their own learning. These strategies encourage critical thinking and lifelong learning.

- Facts are rarely presented in isolation.
- Knowledge is related to the lives and experiences of students.
- Teachers make a practice of explaining how assignments are related to one another, how they continuously build on one another.
- Work is challenging, demanding that students stretch themselves and take academic risks.
- Creativity, expression, and analysis are essential components.
- Discussion of challenges to the status quo, present and past, is frequent.
- Students are encouraged to question.
- Students are given choices and required to present original solutions.
- Learning to write is a process. Writing to learn is supported.
- Textbook knowledge is validated or challenged with other resources.
- Artwork is supplemental.
- Students have freedom of movement and access to resources in support of their learning.
- Initiative, inquisitiveness, and creativity are encouraged.

Strategy One: KWL Revisited

One of the most effective strategies, and one not used nearly enough, is KWL (what I Know, what I Want to know, and what I Learned). During my years in the classroom, and now in my work with teachers, I've expanded on it to incorporate what I've learned about how the brain works. I'm also constantly changing how I use this strategy so the students do more of the work and learn more, and the teacher does less.

Step One: Background Knowledge

We learn based on what we already know. Therefore, it's important to know what the students already know and then to build on their prior knowledge. They frequently know more than they think they know and feel very empowered when you ask them what they already know before you begin imparting what you know. When you begin your lesson without inquiring about and then acknowledging what students are bringing with them, the implication is that you assume students know little or nothing. Validating that students have knowledge encourages them to expand their knowledge base.

Select the topic or concept for study mindfully. Is this topic important enough for students to spend time studying? Is this concept essential to continued learning? Provide a brief introduction. For instance: *We're going to be exploring point of view as it applies to literature, history, politics, even the gathering of scientific data. To better understand how each of us reads the world, let's begin with what we know about zoos and animals in the zoo.*

Divide a sheet of paper into three columns (see Figure 9–1). Instruct students to list everything they know about zoos and the animals in them in the first column. In the second column have them list everything they think they know about zoos and zoo animals, but are not absolutely sure. (I suggest to students that they think of the first column being what they are absolutely sure of and would be willing to bet their prized possession on, and the second column being what they think they know but wouldn't bet their allowance on.) In the third column, they begin to wonder.

What I know for sure	What I think I know, not so sure	What I wonder about
Zoos save species	Animals don't like cages	Are zoo animals content?
Elephants are the favorite attraction	Crocodiles and alligators come from the same place	How did the very first zoo begin? Who thought of it?

FIGURE 9–1
Background Knowledge

Students begin by working individually. They each list at least five entries in each of the first two columns and several *I wonders* in the third. After a few minutes they turn to a nearby student and compare their lists, adding or deleting some of the facts they've written or moving them from the *I know* to the *I think* columns or the other way around. Together they might expand the *I wonder* column. From this pairing they create two new lists, negotiating between them the facts on each. The *know for sure* list tends to grow while the *I think* list shrinks. The *I wonder* column expands.

After the pair-share, depending on the time, we move to a small-group discussion, more items added, more items moved from the *I know* column to the *I think* column and vice versa. The teacher is the cheerleader, pushing students to really dig deeply into their prior knowledge, what they might have read, or heard, or experienced about zoos and zoo animals. We conclude with a whole-class brainstorm.

Teacher's Strategy Toolbox

There is always a considerable knowledge base in the class. I learn very quickly what I don't have to reteach, leaving more time to extend students' knowledge. I also learn about students' misconceptions and can address those in a timely manner. Sometimes there is sufficient collective knowledge to move to the next topic without more investigation.

The Twenty-Four-Hour Blast: Extending Collective Knowledge

Once students have reminded themselves of all they know about the topic, we sometimes do a twenty-four-hour blast. If we are going to continue the study and complete major projects, I don't want the final products to be filled with easy-to-derive facts. I want the students' research to go much deeper. Therefore, we'll spend a day, or class period, on the Blast. Depending upon the instructional goal, I send students to the classroom Internet (when it's available) or to other resources I've compiled in advance, or to the library. The instruction is to return with additional information on the topic that is not already in our lists. I want to get the quickly acquired knowledge out of the way so that it doesn't become the final learning, just a piece of the process. Students respond favorably to this challenge.

It's within every student's ability to gather one or more additional facts. The Blast also allows for differentiated instruction—some students will bring exotic facts they've spent hours uncovering—they always push my own knowledge base; others will be content with one or two additional bits of information they derived from the first website they visited. There are multiple benefits to the class on the whole. First, the students are the givers of the knowledge, not the teacher. Students are often surprised by how much they know and how adept they are at gathering more information; they feel validated as learners and empowered to teach other students. Every time they recall information, retention increases. And—I love this part—the teacher hasn't done all the work.

Step Two: The Inquiry Phase

Based on what we collectively know, we start looking at the gaps in our knowledge. What do all these isolated facts say? What do they mean? What is significant about this body of information? What do we want to know more about? What are we already wondering about? Students then generate questions for further study. *Why is there so much controversy around zoos and caging animals? How do zoos help to prevent animal* extinction? Are zoos responsible for more animals being killed or captured, for the disappearance of whole species? What is my individual responsibility for protecting zoos, or for closing them? Why do some people seem to love animals more than they love people? Is mankind more important than the animal kingdom? Is it okay to experiment on animals to save human life? All of these questions came from students. The questions the class develops, with some assistance from me, are usually more complex than the *I wonders* students initially write. Students really do wonder about all sorts of things; they do want to know and to learn.

The rest of the study is driven by the student inquiries. Students might work individually or in groups as they investigate the questions they chose. Higher motivation is one of the direct benefits of choice. Differentiation is a natural by-product. The variety of inquiry questions that derive from this brainstorming process is always much richer than I can possibly think of on my own. Because original thinking is so highly valued in the twenty-first-century workplace, providing opportunities for students to develop investigations is extremely important.

Final Projects

Students develop a plan for both researching their questions (notice that these are all open-ended questions—less susceptible to direct plagiarism) and for presenting their findings. I provide guidelines that include the minimum number of citations required and suggestions for where to find resource materials. I conference with students around how to present their findings. I follow their progress and offer assistance when they are stuck. But since the work is driven by the students' interest, I don't have to spend time on motivation. The time allocated to the research and presentations is driven by the course content, the overarching instructional goal, and the students' interest. Some of these projects last two days, some continue for weeks.

For this unit, since my goal was to study point of view, I kept the projects, including the research piece, to just a few days, and although it seems like we've gone a long way around, we did come back to our initial goal. Our collected facts about zoos and zoo animals were presented at the outset, but what we did with those facts, how and what we researched, and even how we presented our findings, led us to very different conclusions about the efficacy of zoos. We broadened our discussion and were able to explore point of view, bias in reporting, how facts can yield multiple interpretations. There was no boredom, no worksheets, no disengaged students—and I didn't do all the work.

Students knew in advance that our goal was to understand point of view. Studying zoos and animals was the vehicle.

We could have studied a myriad of topics to get to the same concept. I chose something that I thought would capture students' interest, that already had my interest (my reading of *Life of Pi*). Point of view met the criteria for a concept worthy of the students' efforts. When we understand there are multiple perspectives we can be compassionate of others, develop empathy, open ourselves to the complexity of issues, be persuasive, challenge policy, and be active participants in a democratic society.

Minilessons

Minilessons during the inquiry phase support the students' work. I gave a short lesson on how to cite works used, including an example of EndNote, a software program that creates Works Cited. (Most teachers are still adhering to teaching MLA format, but this software can put the Works Cited into any of more than five dozen formats, so why go any other route? We need to be aware of and use twenty-first-century technology. I'm now learning to use voice-activated software.) Another lesson was on using the Internet to determine the reliability of sources. We spent some whole-class time on writing our research plans. No lesson exceeded twenty minutes, the absolute limit for a lecture. Several times I asked students to take a short break from their group work so I could respond to questions from students that kept surfacing.

The classroom was lively. Students were in and out of their seats to find information from books and the Internet, to compare what they were doing with others, and to rehearse their presentations. Some added artwork, original drawings, photos from the Internet, three-dimensional figures, even plastic animals from children's play sets. Students were praised for their inquisitiveness and applauded by their peers for their creativity.

When we began reading literature selections from our anthology, the questions continued about point of view, about authenticity and reliability of the narrator. They got it! In order to deeply embed important concepts, you have to spend the time; you'll find it's worth it.

Strategy Two: Interactive Reading

The Interactive Reading or Reciprocal Teaching strategy evolved from a study by Palascar and Brown (1984). They examined the skills that successful readers regularly used when reading text. Because reading is invisible—you can see pages turning and eyes moving but the activity is happening inside the head—you can't teach reading through an apprentice model in the same way one would learn to be a plumber. Palascar and Brown made the invisible reading process visible.

Successful readers regularly:

- summarize,
- find the main idea,
- reread,
- question for clarification,
- question more deeply for implication,
- make predictions, and
- think about the significance of what they are reading.

While many students are natural readers who regularly and easily apply these strategies, many do not. Some students read the same way they watch television. Television viewing requires almost no audience participation. The characters and action on the screen continue whether you are actively engaged or not. Not so for reading. In order to comprehend text, you must be actively involved. Interactive reading strategies teach students how to get actively involved with the text. You will find that this strategy is applicable to both print and nonprint text such as artworks and film.

Teaching the Strategy

Students fold a piece of paper into four columns (see Figure 9–2 on page 110). I teach the strategy before applying it to a text we are studying. For the introduction to interactive reading I begin with a very simple text like the one below. Many of you might consider this text to be too simplistic for a secondary classroom, but I assure you it is not. My purpose in selecting a basic text is so that we can focus on the process and not be distracted by having to actually interpret a text. Feel free to change the sample as you please.

Sample text: Four ducks crossed the pond.

This line of text doesn't lend itself to summary, it's so short, but we can extract a main idea (see Figure 9–3). Students each write one or two clarifying questions. These are questions whose answers can be

Main Idea/Summary	Clarifying Questions	Other Questions	Predictions

FIGURE 9–2 Reading Strategy

found in the text. Students write level 2 and level 3 questions—extending into and beyond the text. Finally, students make predictions, based on the text they have already read, about what will happen next.

Main Idea/ Summary	Clarifying Questions	Other Questions	Predictions
Duck movement	How many ducks? What did they cross?	Why did they cross? Was this a family of ducks? What did they find on the other side?	Ducks get shot by hunter. Picnickers feed the ducks.

FIGURE 9–3
Example of Reading Strategy

We continue reading the text.

> Once on the other side, the ducks, a mother duck and her three ducklings, quack loudly until the picnickers feed them.

In the next row on their chart students again complete the main idea or summary. They ask more level 1, 2, and 3 questions. They make another prediction. They also check to see if their prior questions have been answered in the additional text (see Figure 9–4). They want to know if their predictions were correct and cheer one another for predicting accurately. The additional text may or may not answer our questions or validate our predictions.

Main Idea/ Summary	Clarifying Questions	Other Questions	Predictions
Duck movement	How many ducks? What did they cross?	Why did they cross? Was this a family of ducks? What did they find on the other side?	Ducks get shot by hunter. Picnickers feed the ducks.
Ducks cross and eat.	What kind of ducks? What happened when they quacked?	Were these city ducks or country ducks? Where was the papa duck? Did they ever find their own food or have they become domesticated?	The ducks will stay on the grass with the picnickers. More ducks and pigeons will come. One rowdy child will throw stones at them.

FIGURE 9–4
Example of Reading Strategy

Teacher's Strategy Toolbox

111

We continue reading the text (see Figure 9–5):

> The mother duck flapped her wings and chased away the picnickers who were moving too close to her ducklings. She protected her offspring.

Main Idea/ Summary	Clarifying Questions	Other Questions	Predictions
Duck movement	How many ducks? What did they cross?	Why did they cross? Was this a family of ducks? What did they find on the other side?	Ducks get shot by hunter. Picnickers feed the ducks.
Ducks cross and eat.	What kind of ducks? What happened when they quacked?	Were these city ducks or country ducks? Where was the papa duck? Did they ever find their own food or have they become domesticated?	The ducks will stay on the grass with the picnickers. More ducks and pigeons will come. One rowdy child will throw stones at them.
Mother duck protects young.	What did the mother duck do to the picnickers? What did she do for her young ducklings?	Are all wild animals protective? Why did the mother duck fear for her ducklings?	The picnickers would get rowdy. The picnickers protected the ducks. The ducks left for the pond.

Using the Strategy to Improve Comprehension

Have you ever read to the end of a page or chapter and not known what you read? It happens to our low-performing students all the time. They aren't able to make sense of the text, but they read on anyway. Although they can read the words, and they don't need phonics training, they don't understand what they've read. You can't possibly engage students in a meaningful discussion if they haven't even understood the basic facts in the text. We teach comprehension by unpacking the text, by explicitly teaching the strategies that successful readers continually employ.

Summarizing text teaches students to omit less important details and to focus on the main action or ideas. Extracting the *main idea*, which is different from summarizing, focuses on the overarching meaning in the text. These are important, high-level skills. After students have attempted to either summarize or extract the main idea, the teacher can paraphrase if necessary.

Clarifying questions, although not very interesting, are extremely important. We often assume that students "got the facts" and move immediately to level 2 and 3 questions. We're then distressed because the ensuing discussion is vapid. Before uncovering implications and significance, we have to make sure that students have the facts, the basic information. They need to know how many ducks crossed what, where they went, the ducks' relationship to one another, what they did; the facts, just the facts. I have students ask one another the clarifying questions and then read the answers as the information appears in the original text. Students need to return to the text, to learn to read what is actually there. Don't move on until the facts have all been stated and everyone understands that this text is about a duck family crossing the pond. It's the clarifying questions that ensure that students have access and understanding of the literal text, which form the support for moving into deeper readings of the text. This is the reading phase.

Level 2 and 3 Questions

Students need to learn how to ask questions that uncover the implications and significance of the text. For example, in a political speech one asks why one word was chosen over another. What is the function of repetition? Is this an argument based on facts or one that appeals to our emotions? As teachers we are used to asking the questions and calling upon students to respond. In forming the questions we deepen our own understanding. Teaching students to ask the questions strengthens their learning and their engagement. The brain seeks to make sense of the world, to find answers to questions. When students ask the questions themselves they are more motivated to read for the answers.

Prediction

Strong readers predict what's coming and then read to learn whether their prediction is correct. When we read with purpose, to answer questions we've posed, to test our predictions, then comprehension improves. Students with weak prediction skills have difficulty with cause and effect. Not only do they have trouble learning and remembering the causes of WWII, for example, they also have difficulty understanding the consequences of their behavior—cause and effect. Prediction is a skill that can, and should be, explicitly taught. Logical predictions flow from the facts and evidence we already have. For example, if the text states that "Four ducks crossed the pond," predicting that they would get to the other side is logical. It may not be accurate, they may fly away before reaching the other side, but it is a logical prediction nevertheless. To predict, however, that there are six tennis shoes on the side of the lake, is not logical, although it may be true. It cannot be derived from the text. Initially, students may make some wild predictions. Ask what they are basing their predictions upon. Insist that predictions are grounded in the text.

We have some fun with the predictions. Students applaud one another for correctly predicting what follows. Some prediction is based on what you understand about a character's personality. Sometimes a literary figure acts in a manner that students believe is out of character. That opens the way for another discussion that in turn leads to deeper reading and enhanced comprehension.

The Goal

Once you have taught this strategy to the whole class, students can work in groups to uncover text they are studying. Each group member takes a turn at being the facilitator while the remaining group members complete the chart for each section of text. Some students will need more practice than others. You can assist struggling readers with a bookmark (see Figure 9–6) they can refer to on a regular basis.

I want to make a comment here about Interactive Reading, sometimes referred to as Reciprocal Teaching. The strategy is taught as a complete entity indicating that all four parts of the strategy, Summarizing or Main Idea, Clarifying Questions, Other Questions, and Predictions, must be used for the strategy to be effective. Nothing could be further from the truth.

Each part of this strategy has merit and although it can be used in total, it can also be used effectively as separate strategies. For instance, for some text, particularly nonfiction, prediction is not always applicable. You might want to stress recall, or ask about implications for the future, or relate to something they have read or studied before.

FIGURE 9–6
Interactive Reading
Bookmark

Interactive Reading

Summarize
What is the main idea?

What are the facts?
Ask clarifying questions.

What does this imply?
What does it mean?
Is this significant?
How does it relate to . . . ?

What's going to happen next?
What do I expect to learn?
Did my question(s) get answered?

I remind students that being able to extract a main idea from an extended text is very beneficial for studying. You may not want to reread, but if you review the main ideas from each paragraph you have reinforced the learning and prepared for continued study or assessment.

As with KWL, once you understand how each part of the strategy aids student comprehension, motivation, and learning, then you've expanded your teacher's toolbox and can assist more students more effectively.

Teacher's
Strategy Toolbox

Strategy Three: The Squeeze

This is one of my most favorite strategies. I use it with teachers as well as with my students and am always delighted with the results, as are they. The Squeeze strategy is fun, empowers students to be creative, requires cooperation and negotiation, deepens understanding, allows for presentation, and gets everyone engaged in academic talk.

Effective instruction provides frequent opportunities for students to engage in academic discourse—to talk about their learning, about the text, to problem solve, to plan and evaluate. Classrooms where high-quality academic work is the norm are noisy, filled with accountable talk. The Squeeze strategy gets students to talk about what they are learning.

Getting Started

Select a text for study, print or nonprint. Divide students into groups (four per group is ideal). Assign a section of text, the same text, or different but related text, to each group. Each group selects a Summarizer, Verifier, Squeezer, and Recorder/Presenter. All group members read the assigned text.

The Roles

The *Summarizer* orally summarizes the text portion.

The *Verifier* listens intently for accuracy and to determine if the Summarizer included details that could be omitted from the summary, or if there are details that need to be included but weren't. The Verifier restates the summary including any necessary changes.

The *Squeezer* has read the text, listened to the Summarizer and the Verifier, and now reduces the text portion to ten words. You can allow for more or fewer words depending upon the complexity and length of the text portion. However, in my experience a ten-word limit is sufficient for most texts. You can also decide if the ten words can be reported serially or if they need to be in a complete sentence(s).

The *Recorder* writes the Squeeze and presents it to the rest of the class. I usually have the Recorder write on an overhead transparency or a strip of adding-machine tape.

Having an audience of their peers motivates students to refine their squeeze, to correctly use the conventions, to stretch their vocabulary. A lighthearted competitive spirit prevails. Students are not assigned points or grades; the Squeeze is a learning activity, not designed to sort students into those who can and those who can't.

The Presentation

Each group presents its squeeze to the rest of the class. If the text portions are sequential, then groups present in order. When groups are reading different sections of text, I require students to write down each of the squeezes, which together comprise a summary of the total reading and is an excellent prereading activity. When the class goes on to read the entire text, students will already have some background information. Comprehension goes up because vocabulary has been grappled with, main ideas have been identified, the text has been previewed. Students now have background knowledge that connects to their new learning. Even struggling students are able to understand the bulk of the text.

If every group has read the same text, then presentations may be random. We learn that not every group reports the same main idea even though they read the same text. The diversity of findings leads to deep discussion about what a reader brings to the text (back to point of view). We discuss how reading the same text may yield different information for different readers. This is another rich and worthwhile discussion that has deep implications for analysis and interpretation of text, print and nonprint.

Why It Works

Even though students are assigned distinct tasks, the group takes ownership. They know in advance that they will present their Squeeze to the entire class, not just to the teacher. Peer pressure requires them to do their best work, to be grammatically correct, and to write legibly. Group members carefully examine the text to extract the main idea. They use, without teacher prodding, dictionaries and thesauri to find the best words with which to present their squeeze. They negotiate and compromise in order to reach consensus. Adolescents are social beings, they need time for talk. This strategy requires academic, focused discussion around ideas, lots of accountable talk.

There is an element of competition, and there's fun. Students may ask to use one or two aditional words. I respond that each extra word costs a $1, a contribution to our class fund. Some groups use fewer words and then ask if they can sell their extra word(s) to another group. We all laugh about these requests, I never take money. Students have choice, they belong to a group, there are no wrong answers or competitive grades. What there is, is deep investigation of text.

The Squeeze doesn't stand alone, it's part of an extended teaching sequence. It works well as an Into, Through, or Beyond strategy. (Into the text; during the text; or after, beyond the completion of the text.) It can be used to summarize an entire unit, to extract essential learnings. The Squeeze can be redesigned as a question rather than a statement—what question does this text answer?

As with the other strategies offered in this chapter, the Squeeze requires active student participation. Students are constructing their learning, and we know that retention is highest when students are active participants. And, although the teacher selects the text, there is no lecturing. The ideas and information are presented by the students to the students. Teachers ensure accuracy. Be prepared for alternate, but still accurate interpretations of text you may not have considered before. Student learning goes up when we yield the stage.

Strategy Four: Say, Mean, Matter

I first learned this strategy from my colleague Shelia Sutton, who said she learned it from teacher/author Kelly Gallagher, who said he got it from a workshop with professor/author Sheridan Blau. And Blau may have first learned this strategy from someone else as well. I continually learn new strategies in order to expand my repertoire, keep my students interested and engaged, and keep myself from being bored. This reading comprehension strategy has widespread use for fiction and nonfiction, for print and nonprint text. It directs students to examine the text's surface features and to also uncover the deeper meanings. We read for basic information, but we also read to understand and to change the world. What begins as a strategy becomes a way of reading all text, including people.

Say: What does the text say? What is the information presented? What are the facts as presented? (This is what the clarifying questions in Interactive Reading seek to uncover.) Consider: What is the character/person saying? What is the character/person doing?

Mean: What does this information mean? What is the implication inherent within the text? What thoughts and emotions does the text evoke? Consider: What does it mean when the character/person takes this action? Says these words? What is the motivation, the intention?

Matter: So what? We have the facts and we have the implications, what does it all matter? What is the significance of this text? How does it impact the rest of the text/novel/story/work? How does it impact the world? What challenges can we present to the text or because of the text?

The following example is taken from my opening letter to students at the beginning of a course or semester:

Text: All students are expected to accomplish the standards established for this course. Because we recognize that not all students enter with the same skills, some students may require more time and may need to submit several revisions of their work. Every student is encouraged to revise and resubmit their work for reconsideration as often as necessary. The ultimate goal is to master the standards.

Say: The teacher said everyone has to meet the goals. You can redo your work until you get there.

Mean: This means that the quality of the student work counts. This also means that you have to redo your work until it is your best.

Matter: This matters because the teacher wants everyone to be accomplished. The teacher is willing to reread and regrade your work until you do it well. The teacher understands that you may not have the same skills, but she's there as long as you need her to help you to achieve them. It also means that shoddy, incomplete, or missing work is not acceptable.

Model and Practice

We learn through example and practice. Demonstrate for the whole class the Say, Mean, Matter technique using increasingly complex text, print and nonprint. Allow students to practice in small-group settings. Lead discussions about what happens to their understanding as they practice this strategy. Although we frequently assess what we learn, if we want students to become lifelong learners it's equally important to examine how we learn. Have students create wall posters demonstrating Say, Mean, Matter. Their posters serve as reminders to apply this strategy anytime they are reading a text.

Some of your students will struggle to understand the "matter" portion of this strategy. Don't give up on them. If we expect that they won't ever get it, then we won't support their striving, we'll settle for less than they can do. You'll need to do more modeling and to scaffold and assist when necessary, but don't quit. The excitement on their faces when they realize that they understand the importance of what they are reading, and most will over time, is well worth the combined effort you and your students have expended.

I want to add a note of clarification here. Throughout the section on strategies I've used the terms print and nonprint text. Many of you may not be familiar with the latter term. Nonprint text refers to artworks—painting, sculpture, dance, music, theater, as well as film, commercials, and photographs. Chemists read and study chemical reactions. Artists study form and color. Poets shape their words. This generation is more visual than the last and has more complex data to interpret. Studying nonprint text, in many forms, is equally important to studying print text as we gather information and interpret the world around us. Therefore, studying how to interpret nonprint sources, even how to *read* people, their body language, word choices, and dress, will serve our students well. And, identifying and studying nonprint text adds variety to every discipline and decreases boredom by expanding the possibilities. All students come already equipped with the ability to read nonprint text. Even the youngest children know a frown on their mother's or teacher's face means trouble. Bringing the study of nonprint text into the classroom helps to strengthen this skill.

Strategy Five: Active Reading Symbols

As you've already noticed, a major theme linking all of these featured strategies is their dependence on student involvement and their lack of dependence on the teacher. Active Reading Symbols is another strategy that students can employ with minimal direction.

Creating a student-centered classroom requires continual attention to moving away from the teacher as the source of all knowledge and toward assisting the students as they develop their abilities to create, to investigate, to recall, and to interpret. Student-centeredness is instrumental to seamless classroom management. When students are engaged, when all students have effective strategies they can apply to increase their own learning, then there is not a continual struggle for control of the classroom. The opportunities and motivation for disruptive behavior are reduced.

Instructions

The teacher explains each of the Active Reading Symbols (see Figure 9–7). As students read the assigned text they mark the text with the

FIGURE 9–7
Active Reading
Symbols

Active Reading Symbols

A   I agree

X   I disagree or
     I need help

+   New
     information

?   I need
     clarification
     or
     I wonder
     about

??? I don't get it

!!! Wow

applicable symbol. Initially, students are required to use a minimum number of the symbols depending upon the length and complexity of the text. At the conclusion of the reading the teacher might begin the discussion by saying: Let's begin with what needs clarification. Students have already marked their text and are able to ask for clarification. Instead of responding, the teacher redirects the clarification questions to other students. This sends the message that the teacher is not the only source of information or clarification.

Teacher's Strategy Toolbox

The Symbols

There is nothing sacred about the symbols. Feel free to copy them exactly or alter them to fit your classroom. Create a wall poster students can refer to. Apply them to the reverse side of the Say, Mean, Matter bookmark for easy-to-use reminders. Laminated bookmarks reduce the overuse of handouts and save time and paper.

Strategy Six: Reflective Conversation Questions and Statements

When I first began working with teachers seeking National Board Certification, I thought that when I put them into groups to examine one another's writing, they would be on task, provide constructive criticism, offer appropriate praise, and assist one another in improving their writing. Wrong! Four or five people—even teachers—sitting together do not necessarily make for a strong learning community. We all need to be taught how to participate in a group. I also realized from watching my teacher-students that many times my children's groups didn't work well either. That's when I began to teach my students how to talk to one another so work can progress. I came across some of these Reflective Conversation Questions and Statements during a National Board Support training session and have since altered them, expanded them, and learned from others what works and what doesn't in different situations. I teach them in a reduced version, as sentence starters, to primary students and use them in Socratic seminars, for peer revision sessions, and to teach active listening skills.

There are three distinct features to these sentence starters, each with its own purpose: paraphrasing, clarifying, and mediating.

Paraphrasing
So . . .
In other words . . .
What I'm hearing then . . .
What I hear you saying . . .
From what I hear you say . . .
I'm hearing many things . . .
As I listen to you I'm hearing . . .

We use paraphrasing to make sure we understand what the speaker has said. It is a loose form of summarizing. Paraphrasing attempts to capture the essence of what the speaker has said. It is also an opportunity for the speaker to learn what the listeners have heard, sometimes very different from what was intended. The technique works equally well whether you are listening to one or more speakers or studying nonprint text. (What I'm seeing in this sketch is . . .) Students are instructed to use the sentence starters to verify that they are getting the intended message correctly from the speaker.

Clarifying

Would you tell me a little more about . . . ?
Let me see if I understand . . .
I'd be interested in hearing more about . . .
It'd help me understand if you'd give me an example of . . .
So, are you saying/suggesting . . . ?
Tell me what you mean when you . . .
Tell me how that idea is like (different from) . . .
To what extent . . . ?
I'm curious to know more about . . .
I'm intrigued by . . .
I'm interested in . . .
I wonder . . .

Clarifying questions seek to deepen understanding, to fill in the gaps. When used for the purpose of peer editing they form a framework for getting student writers-researchers to respond to an audience. They are a way to probe for more information without saying, "That's dumb! What are you talking about?" or other unhelpful remarks students make to one another. While teachers working together in groups may be more polite and avoid these types of remarks, they are more prone to assuming that if something the presenting teacher is saying is unclear it must be because *they* are not as smart; the fault lies within them rather than with the presenting teacher. As a result, they tend not to ask clarifying questions at all. With both younger and adult students, reviewing the clarifying question starters and encouraging their use leads to better writing and deeper understanding. Clarifying questions are excellent for peer editing. They also help students to move their research into areas where the audience has genuine interest and to develop characters more deeply. When we're writing position papers, students challenge one another's ideas through paraphrasing techniques.

Mediating

What's another way you might . . . ?

What would it look like if . . . ?

What do you think would happen if . . . ?

How was . . . different from (like) . . . ?

What sort of an impact do you think . . . ?

What criteria do you use to . . . ?

When have you done something like . . . before?

What do you think . . .?

How did you decide . . . (come to that conclusion)?

What might you see happening in your essay if . . . ?

Mediating questions or statements come from cognitive coaching. Instead of seeking to provide answers to something the speaker may be struggling with, mediating questions push the speaker/presenter to stretch his own ideas, to search for alternatives and try them out in the group. Those skilled in asking mediating questions can extend learning for the presenter and for themselves.

Getting Started

Determine in advance which sentence starters or questions are applicable to your students at this time. For younger children I put two or three choices on index cards for each reference. For secondary students, the complete sheet, or a slightly abridged one, works well.

Introduce the sentence starters or questions and briefly explain the importance and basic use of each type. In groups, have the students read them one at a time, taking turns, employing tone and emphasis. Listening to the students is itself a fun experience and gets them more comfortable with the phrases.

I don't use all the sections all the time, just as I don't use all four parts of Interactive Reading all the time. I sometimes instruct students to focus on clarifying questions, especially during peer-editing sessions. For Socratic seminars we might use paraphrasing and clarifying questions. If we're working on presentations, we will use mediating phrases most often to explore possibilities the presenter might not have thought of before. When making choices, consider your instructional goals and then select the techniques that are most appropriate. Until they become second nature, I instruct students to refer to the Reflective Conversation Questions and Statements when working in their groups.

As students become more skilled with these tools, they can select what and when to use them. Keeping a chart on the classroom wall serves as a handy reference for you and for the students.

Knowing how to effectively, and gently, critique another's work is a skill that is seldom taught. We put students into teams, we tell them to edit one another's work, we admonish them when they aren't listening to the speaker but focusing on their own comments, then assume they can do this without more instruction.

Closing Remarks

Teaching the strategies included in this chapter takes time. But when students own a variety of strategies, and can make choices about when and how to apply them, then they take charge of their learning.

One of my first observations when I became a teacher was that *teaching was hard work, definitely more difficult and time-consuming than anything I had done before.* The heavy secondary school workload, the numbers of students we teach each day, and the sometimes difficult school conditions all contribute to teacher burnout. Teachers leave the profession in alarming numbers—50 percent in the first five years. Some remain but are stuck in fixed routines, boring for their students and for themselves. In order to sustain vibrancy and enthusiasm, we need to be much smarter about our work, to question everything we do and everything we ask of students. Academic success, all success, derives from a combination of Effort plus Effective Strategies. The most effective teachers give their students the tools to support their own learning. The strategies highlighted in this section are designed to do just that—turn the tools of learning over from teacher to student, from master craftsman to apprentice.

Pause and Reflect

Review the list of domesticating and liberating strategies included above. What strategies do you currently rely on? What would you like to add? Which strategies do you currently use that should be in the trash can? What are the challenges in adding a new strategy to your repertoire? What are the benefits? Give one—get one: Ask a colleague to describe a strategy he uses effectively, then share one you find helpful to students.

Chapter Ten

Teacher Traits
What Makes a Great Teacher?

Care more than others think wise.
Risk more than others think safe.
Dream more than others think practical.
Expect more than others think possible.

■Howard Schultz, *Pour Your Heart into It*

I enjoy reading business journals and management books. They help me maintain a focus beyond the classroom, the venue where our students will spend the majority of their lives. In December 2001 I read an article about teaching in *Fast Company* magazine, a business journal. The primary audience for this article was business leaders, but its message applies especially well to pre-K–12 classroom teachers. Author Chuck Salter believes that great leaders are also great teachers and great teachers are powerful leaders. After all, aren't you leading a roomful of young people every day? Salter defines what he considers great teaching. I kept the article because his findings mirror my own and fit perfectly with the theme of this book: effective teaching requires turning the learning over to students.

Speech making (lecturing) and giving orders (instructions), Salter points out, are more akin to dictating than they are to leading, and thus not indicative of great leadership, or of great teaching. When the primary mode of delivery is lecture followed by direction giving, you don't have great teaching. You also don't have high levels of learning. Besides, even good lecturing, I like to remind teachers, is hard work; lecturing is performance at its most demanding. I avoid it whenever I can.

Here are the sixteen teaching and leading traits Slater identified, followed by my comments.

1. It's Not About You; It's About Them

This book has undergone several working titles. In my lighter mood I called it, "It Is About Them!" If education is all about you, the teacher, you're working way too hard and your students aren't working or learning nearly enough. Banish the concept of teacher as designated expert or, as one of my students said, *knowledge dictator*. The more students depend upon you, the less likely they are to develop independent thinking skills. Dependent learners don't take academic risks, nor do they think creatively. They measure productivity by what the teacher wants without internalizing measurements for high productivity or high quality—very important traits for success in the twenty-first-century marketplace.

During my education credential program the professors stressed lesson planning—what the teacher is going to do. When we shift our focus from us to them and ask, "What are my students going to do today?" we get remarkably different, and better, results.

2. Study Your Students

You can't know what and how to teach if you don't know your audience. What works in one class may not work well in another. What does this set of students bring with them and what are their goals? You won't teach effectively if you don't have the answers to these questions. Check out Chapter Nine, "Teacher's Strategy Toolbox," for ways of getting to know what your students know.

3. Students Take Risks When Teachers Create a Safe Environment

We've spent an entire chapter on establishing the classroom environment (Chapter Two). I want to add that speaking the truth, being honest, and cheating and plagiarizing less begin with students' academic safety. You are the classroom environment.

4. Great Teachers Exude Passion as Well as Purpose

Increasingly, teachers are juggling federal, state, district, and school mandates that threaten to crowd out any opportunities for teaching to our passions. Find a way. In all of the mandated curriculums I've studied, there is some wiggle room. Students learn so much more when we teach what we are passionate about. We don't just transfer knowledge, we transfer passion. Those who are passionate about learning or doing anything are more likely to be successful—and Starbuck's chairman Howard Schultz agrees. If you absolutely cannot find wiggle room beyond the mandates, create some. It's easier to apologize after the fact, should you get caught, than to ask for permission. Besides, who can argue if your students are learning more and enjoying their education?

5. Students Learn When Teachers Show Them How Much They Need to Learn

Begin with the end in mind (see Chapter Four). Tell students in advance what you are teaching and why; how what they will be learning is important to their lives, now and in the future. They can't follow you if they don't know where you're going. Teach goal setting. Students need to evaluate where they are now, compare their current status to their goals, and then set the pace for their own achievement. Without understanding their own learning gaps, they won't be motivated to fill them. You can spend your time pushing them along, or you can lead them. Great teachers are great leaders.

6. Keep It Clear Even If You Can't Keep It Simple

Begin with where your students are and tell them where you're all going, but teach in increments. Don't move forward until they've mastered the first steps. If they see the gap as too great, they won't even try. If the lesson is too simple, they'll be unmotivated and bored. If they're not getting it, whatever the *it* of the moment is, ask yourself what you can do differently. Your students may need more time, may lack some background knowledge on which this new concept is dependent, or may not understand how this bit of information fits with what came before or what will come later. Check frequently for understanding before moving on. The challenge is to differentiate enough for all students; how do you balance the needs of the slower learners with those who gulp down whole new skills and information? All their learning doesn't have to happen under your direct tutelage. Assign additional tutoring, engage the parents, call on your school's resources. Students will differentiate their own responses if the assessments are more open-ended. Those who are more able will go deeper and do more when the assessments measure the quality of work, not just the quantity.

7. Practice Vulnerability Without Sacrificing Credibility

You don't have to always be right. You certainly don't need to know all the answers to all of the questions, asked or not yet asked. Watch a teen's posture change when you respond to one of his or her questions with, "What a great question! I don't know the answer. How can we find out?" When students ask thoughtful questions, you know they are highly engaged. Acknowledging that the student's question is a great one builds their self-esteem, and you don't have to fake it. You're also modeling lifelong learning—yours.

8. Teach from the Heart

If following a script worked and led all students to achieve at high levels, we'd all follow scripts. But they don't work very well, as we discover every day. You have to know your students, care about each of them, monitor what they're learning, and commit yourself to adding value. You have to teach what and how you are. You can't leave heart outside the door.

9. Repeat the Important Points

Depth, not breadth. Determine what is important and then strive to help students master the important points. Provide practice time; approach the same material from multiple perspectives. This is not the same as saying that you should give directions five times over, orally, on the board, on the overhead, in a handout, and orally again—not at all. But approaching the learning goal from several angles can deepen the learning. You'll know they have it if you watch for the lightbulbs going on.

10. Good Teachers Ask Good Questions

Study Chapter Nine, "Teacher's Strategy Toolbox," for a discussion about the three basic levels of questioning. *What would that look like if . . . ?* is an excellent follow-through question. Questions are powerful ways to move students into more critical thinking. Questioning worked wonderfully well for Socrates. Asking students what makes for a good learning environment is more effective than posting a predetermined set of teacher rules. Asking what your clients—the students—want to know gets them engaged in the learning process. It's more difficult to learn to ask questions than it is to summarize and deliver information; this is true for teachers as well as for students.

I'm frequently surprised by the responses I get when I prod students to ask the questions; I always get more than I anticipated. During one of my precandidate classes for teachers working on National Board Certification, I discovered that most of the teachers struggled with asking questions about what they were reading. There's no set formula, but the Reflective Conversation Questions and Statements contained in Chapter Nine are a good starting point. Be kind to yourself as you incorporate questioning beyond the "known response" type; it takes practice. You, too, have to feel safe to venture into the unknown.

11. You're Not Passing Out Information

What information do you provide students that they can't glean on their own, with your excellent guidance? Straight information can be acquired from a variety of resources, including the Internet. Great teaching is about process, probing for understanding, pushing students to challenge what they read and hear and see, and encouraging them to check their sources. You're teaching them how to think on their own, not just stuffing their heads full of factlets.

12. Stop Talking and Start Listening

Ask students to report on what they've learned through strategies like the Squeeze (Chapter Nine) rather than providing them with an outline of key points. Help them to ask inquiry-level questions and to do the research necessary to answer them. Learn how to increase *wait-time*—the amount of time you allow between asking a question and waiting for a response. (As I said before, the average teacher waits less than three seconds before answering her own question or moving on to another student.) Work toward a three-minute lapse. Allow for accountable talk time between students then listen in on their conversations. Plan your teaching based on what you learn from students, from their words and from their work. Listening to students demonstrates that you care about them and respect their ideas.

13. Learn What to Listen For

When you listen, you'll have clues to students' interests, to their misconceptions, and to what they've mastered. You'll know about their reasoning skills, about how they question one another, what frustrates them, and what makes them feel successful. When you paraphrase their words, as in, "I heard Margaret say that . . . " you're validating all students, and getting their attention.

14. Let Your Students Teach Each Other

And let them teach you. Well-designed small groups multiply the number of teachers in the room. I read somewhere that only 17 percent of what students learn in school happens in the classroom. Students learn from their peers, from outside sources, from other adults. When you structure the task and take the time to teach students how to work effectively together, you've reduced the time you're onstage and provided time for more interactive learning opportunities. You can say, *I think this is true, let's check it out*, but when you are adamant that you're correct, that there's only one way to respond, then you've shut off any further inquiry or thinking on the students' part. We have to let go of believing that we are the final authority on anything. There's more to learn about everything you already know—that's why learning lasts your whole life, and is never completed, and why teachers who continue to learn don't burn out.

15. Avoid Using the Same Approach for Everyone

Not everyone responds well to any single approach. The reality of the classroom may dictate that you can't orchestrate several strategies at the same time, and that's fine. But you can keep your teacher's toolbox full and use a variety of strategies over time. Watch and listen for what's working with which students. Use strategies, like KWL, that allow for varied student responses.

16. Never Stop Teaching

Learning happens best when there is a relationship between the students and the teacher. You can't teach unless the students believe you care about them, and you can't fake caring. You can't turn off the relationship because it's three o'clock, but you also can't be on twenty-four hours a day. Strike a balance. Allow for occasional after-hours email contacts, especially with parents. Attend a football game or school play, dance at the prom. When you see your students bagging groceries ask the question, if the cans go on top and the tomatoes on the bottom what will I have for dinner? Then laugh with them.

Teacher Traits

Closing Remarks

I study Torah with a rabbi once a month. Once, when I was feeling overwhelmed by all of the Jewish laws—there's 613 of them—I asked the rabbi, Who is closest to God—the person who observes one law or the person who adheres to all 613 mitzvoth? He responded that a person's closeness to God is measured not by the number of laws one maintains but by the direction in which he or she is going. Instead of abandoning the study of Judaism altogether because I felt so overwhelmed by what I didn't know, that explanation gave me permission to take one step at a time.

Becoming a more effective teacher, turning learning over to students, begins wherever you are in your practice, even on step one. Your accomplishment depends on which direction you are traveling.

References

Barth, R. S. 2001. *Learning by Heart*. San Francisco: Jossey-Bass.

California, State of. 1999. *Reading/Language Arts Framework for California Public Schools: Kindergarten Through Grade Twelve*. Sacramento: California Department of Education.

Covey, S. 1998. *The 7 Habits of Highly Effective Teens*. New York: Simon and Schuster.

Erickson, H. L. 1998. *Concept-Based Curriculum and Instruction: Teaching Beyond the Facts*. Thousand Oaks, CA: Corwin Press.

Erwin, J. C. 2003. "Giving Students What They Need." *Educational Leadership* 61 (September): 19–23.

Gardner, H. 1999. *The Disciplined Mind: What All Students Should Understand*. New York: Simon and Schuster.

Goleman, D. 1995. *Emotional Intelligence: Why It Can Matter More Than IQ*. New York: Bantam Books.

Johnson, E. B. 2002. *Contextual Teaching and Learning*. Thousand Oaks, CA: Corwin Press.

Kozminsky, E., and L. Kozminsky. 2003. "Improving Motivation Through Dialogue." *Educational Leadership* 61 (September): 50–53.

Martel, Y. 2003. *Life of Pi*. New York: Harvest Books.

Marzano, R. J. 2003. *What Works in Schools: Translating Research into Action*. Alexandria, VA: Association for Supervision and Curriculum Development.

McGrath, C. 2004. "Not Funnies." *New York Times Magazine*, July 11.

Newemann, F. A., and A. S. Bryk, et al. 2001. *Authentic Intellectual Work or Standardized Tests: Conflict or Coexistence?* Chicago: Consortium on Chicago School Research.

Norton, B. and J. Greco, eds. 2002. *Aiming High: High Schools for the Twenty-First Century*. Sacramento: California Department of Education.

Palmer, P. 1998. *The Courage to Teach: Exploring the Inner Landscape of a Teacher's Life*. San Francisco: Jossey-Bass.

Perkins-Gough, D. 2003. "Creating a Timely Curriculum: A Conversation with Heidi Hayes Jacobs." *Educational Leadership* 61 (4): 12–17.

Robinson, K. 2001. *Out of Our Minds*. Repr., Oxford: Capstone, 2003.

Rosenbaum, J. E. 2001. *Beyond College for All: Career Paths for the Forgotten Half*. New York: Russell Sage Foundation.

Salter, C. 2001. "Attention Class! 16 Ways to Be a Smarter Teacher." *The Fast Company Magazine* (53): 114.

Schultz, H. 1997. *Pour Your Heart into It: How STARBUCKS Built a Company One Cup at a Time*. New York: Hyperion.

Smilkstein, R. 2003. *We're Born to Learn: Using the Brain's Natural Learning Process to Create Today's Curriculum*. Thousand Oaks, CA: Corwin Press.

Sousa, D. D. A. 1995. *How the Brain Learns*. Reston, VA: The National Association of Secondary School Principals.

Strong, R., S. Harvey, M. Perini, and G. Tuculescu. 2003. "Boredom and Its Opposite." *Educational Leadership* 61 (September): 24–29.

Thornburg, D. 2002. *The New Basics: Education and the Future of Work in the Telematic Age*. Alexandria, VA: Association for Supervision and Curriculum Development.

Wiggins, G., and J. McTighe. 1998. *Understanding by Design*. Alexandria, VA: Association for Supervision and Curriculum Development.

Wolk, S. 1998. *A Democratic Classroom*. Portsmouth, NH: Heinemann.

———. 2003. "Hearts and Minds." *Educational Leadership* 61 (September): 14–18.

Wyatt III, R. L, and S. Looper. 1999. *So You Have to Have a Portfolio: A Teacher's Guide to Preparation and Presentation*. Thousand Oaks, CA: Corwin Press.

Index

academic achievement
  challenging assignments and, 42
  classroom management and, 10
  expectations and, 13, 25, 36–37, 71
  grading and, 58–59, 66–67, 87–88
  parents and, 81
  risk-taking and, 25
  student responsibility for, 76–78, 85
  student understanding of causal factors of, 76, 85
academic content standards. *See* standards
academic habits, 83–88
  changing, 83–84
  defined, 83–84
  goal setting, 85
  priorities, 86
  proactivity, 85
  reflection, 88
  renewal, 87–88
  responsibility, 85
  synergy, 87
  understanding others, 86
  win-win attitude, 86
Active Reading Symbols strategy, 120–22
  instructions, 120–21
  symbols, 121–22
advocacy, motivation and, 32
agendas, guidelines for, 15–16
Annenberg Institute for School Reform, 70
assessments, 51–63
  feedback, 54–55
  formative, 53–54
  goals for, 52–53
  grading, 57–60
  mandated, 40–41, 42
  peer editing and correcting, 55–57
  purpose of, 51–52

  questions for, 52–53
  read-arounds, 60–62
  standardized tests, 42–43
  summative, 53–54
assignments
  agendas, 15–16
  differentiating, 37–38
  group correction of, 62
  standards and, 70
at-risk students, 18–19
attention span, 3
audience, 116

background knowledge
  KWL strategy and, 104–6
  learning and, 4
  reading and, 4
backward design, 37
basic knowledge, assessment of, 6–7
behavioral goals, for portfolios, 66, 70–72
behavior rubric, 71–72
beliefs, of teachers, 13–14
bell curve, 57–58
biases, of teachers, 13–14
Blau, Sheridan, 118
books
  in classroom, 12–13
  picture books, 13
book shelves, 12
boredom, 32
brain
  development of, 2
  learning and, 1–8
brain cells, 2
Brown, Ann, 108–9
busy work, 102
California State Frameworks, 44–45
calorie consumption, thinking and, 2

candles, in classroom, 12
Carrol, Lewis, 34
cause and effect
   prediction skills and, 114
   study habits and, 77, 85
celebrations, 26–27
challenging work
   academic achievement and, 42
   motivation and, 2
   value of, 42
choice
   motivation and, 31
   opportunities for, 32
chunking lessons, 3
Cinder Ella, 13
Cinderella, 13
clarifying questions
   in interactive reading, 110–12, 113,
     114
   in learning communities, 122–23
clarity, in student portfolios, 68
class norms, 22, 24
classroom community, 9–11. *See also*
   learning communities
classroom culture, 28
classroom environment, 9–29
   agendas, 15–16
   for at-risk students, 18–19
   books, 12–13
   celebrations, 26–27
   classroom culture, 28
   emotional safety, 3, 25–26
   for gifted students, 19–20
   group norms and, 22, 24
   improving physical space, 11–12
   learning and, 3
   learning communities and, 21–22,
     23
   learning journals, 16–17
   lifelong learning and, 24–25
   motivation and, 31
   music, 12
   organization, 10, 14–15
   raising hands, 17
   reflection, 28–29
   risk-taking and, 127
   routines, 15
   rules and, 20
   sense of space and time, 27–28
   silence and, 20–21
   smells, 12
   teacher attitudes and, 13–14
   win-win atmosphere, 26
classroom management
   classroom monitors and, 17–18

discipline, 17–18
   disruptive behavior, 19
   engagement and, 49
   student achievement and, 10
   teaching strategies and, ix
classroom monitors, 18
community building
   classroom factors, 9–11
community of learners. *See* learning
   communities
competence, self-questioning of,
   76–77
comprehension
   interactive reading and, 112–15
   The Squeeze strategy and, 116–18
conferences, student-led. *See* student-
   led conferences
connections, motivation and, 6
consistency, in student portfolios, 68
Consortium on Chicago School Research,
   70
Contextual Teaching and Learning
   (Johnson), 45
convincing work, in student portfolios,
   68
cool media, 89
cooperative workplace teams, 86
core skills, 39–40
Covey, Sean, 84–88
creative organizations, 28
critical thinking skills, 68, 103–4, 130
curriculum
   mandated assessments, 40–41, 42
   mandated pacing plans, 41–42

democracy, discussion and, 21
D grades, 67
differentiation, 45
   of assignments, 37–38
   in inquiry, 107
   of knowledge collection, 106
   in teaching, 128, 131
Digital-Age Literacy, 39
discipline
   out-of-control students, 17–18
   sheriff-for-the-day, 18
discussion
   encouraging, 20–21
   listening and, 86
domesticating strategies, 102–3

Ed Trust, 36–37
Effective Communication, 40
emotional environment, 3, 25–26
employment, core skills for, 39–40

Enciso, Alfee, 12, 25
EndNote software, 108
end-of-semester/end-of-year portfolio
    reflection, 81, 82
engagement
    classroom management and, 49
    learning journals and, 17
English Language Arts standard
        (California State Framework), 36,
        44
    instructional goals, 66
equipment, organization of, 14–15
essential questions, 43–46
essential understandings, 43–46
expectations, achievement and, 13, 25,
        36–37
external rewards, motivation and, 30

"Failure Bulletin Board," 25
Fast Company magazine, 126
feedback
    limiting, 55
    by peers, 55–57, 57–60
    prescriptive, 54–55
    promptness of, 54
    on student portfolio reflections,
        76–78
    by teacher, 54–55
Final Assessment, 98
final projects, in KWL strategy, 107–8
Finn, Patrick, 102
Fish Bowl strategy, 55–56
Flat Stanley, 13
folders, for portfolios, 65–66
formative assessments, 53–54
Franklin, Benjamin, 83
Friere, Paulo, 102
front-loading, 7
fun, motivation and, 32
future, core skills for, 39–40

Gallagher, Kelly, 118
Gardner, Howard, 2, 22
George Mason University, 101
gifted students, resources for, 19–20
goal setting. *See also* instructional goals
    for interactive reading, 114–15
    by students, 85, 128
grading. *See also* assessments
    academic achievement and, 66–67
    bell-curve distribution, 57–58
    D grades, 67
    district mandates, 59
    final grades
        finality of, 57

inflated self-reporting, 75
    nonacademic skills and, 87–88
    "not yet ready for a grade," 26, 57
    post-secondary achievement and,
        68, 69, 87–88
    promotion and, 81
    purpose of, 51
    required, 58–59
    self-reported, 59–60, 76–77
    standards and, 66–67
    by teachers, 62
    underreported self-reporting, 76–77
group feedback, 55–57
group norms, 22, 24
group work
    cooperative workplace teams, 86
    synergy in, 87

habits, 83–88. *See also* academic habits
    changing, 83–84
    defined, 83–84
    identifying, 84
Harris, Ron, 46
hearing, learning and, 2
Hicks, Steven, 101
High Productivity, 40, 68
hot media, 89

identity, knowing student names,
        10–11
information doubling, 39
inquiry. *See also* questions
    differentiation in, 107
    in KWL strategy, 106–7
    shared, 46–48
instructional goals, 5, 7. *See also* goal
        setting
    "beyond the classroom" applications
        of, 39
    content standards and, 35–36
    designing instruction based on, 37
    for portfolios, 68, 69
    relevance of, 38–37
    student achievement of, 38
    value of, 34–35
instructional strategies. *See* teaching
        strategies
intelligences, multiple, 2, 22
interactive reading, 108–15
    clarifying questions, 110–12, 113,
        114
    comprehension and, 112–15
    goals for, 114–15
    main ideas, 109, 113, 114
    other questions, 111–12, 113, 114

predictions, 111–12, 113–14, 115
summarizing, 109, 113, 114
summary and questions form, 109
teaching, 108–12
interdependence, 45
Internet
knowledge collection using, 106
minilessons on, 108
Inventive Thinking, 39–40

Johnson, Elaine, 45
journals. *See* learning journals

know column, in KWL strategy, 105
knowledge
background, 4, 104–6
basic, assessment of, 6–7
collection of, 106
construction of, 6
"known response" questions, 48
KWL (Know, Want to know, Learn)
strategy, 7, 104–6
background knowledge, 104–6
extending collective knowledge, 106
final projects, 107–8
inquiry phase, 106–7
minilessons, 108

learning
attention span and, 3
background knowledge and, 4
brain and, 1–8
calorie consumption and, 2
classroom environment and, 3
conditions for, 21–22, 23
emotional environment and, 3,
25–26
pleasures of, 1–2
priority and, 2–3
rate of, 4
reading and, 4
relevance and, 3
retention and, 3–4
student reflection on, 27–28
teaching strategies for, 5–7
learning communities
building, 9–12
clarifying questions in, 122–23
encouraging, 21–22
meditating questions in, 123–24
motivation and, 31
paraphrasing in, 122
teaching students to work in,
122–24
learning goals. *See* instructional goals

learning journals, 5, 16–17, 79
value of, 29
learning style, 22
letters, to parents, 92, 93
liberating strategies, 102–4
Liddle, David, 28
lifelong learning, 24–25, 129
Life of Pi (Martel), 46
listening, 86, 130–31
Literacy with an Attitude (Finn), 102
long-term memory, 3–4
Looper, S., 64

main idea, in interactive reading, 109,
113, 114
mandated assessments, 40–41, 42
mandated pacing plans, 41–41
manila folders, for portfolios, 65–66
Martel, Yann, 46
Marzano, Robert, 10
materials and supplies, organizing, 14
Math standards (California State
Framework), 44
Matter, in Say, Mean, Matter Strategy,
118–19
McGrath, Charles, 47
McLuhan, Marshall, 89
McTighe, Jay, 37
Mean, in Say, Mean, Matter Strategy,
116
meditating questions, 123–24
memory
long-term, 3–4
retrieving information from, 5
short-term, 3
mindfulness
defined, xiii
teaching strategies and, xiii–xv
minilessons, in KWL strategy, 108
misconceptions, learning and, 4
MLA style, 108
modeling, portfolio reflection, 73, 76
Monroe High School, Los Angeles, 46
motivation, 30–33
boredom and, 32
challenging material and, 2
conditions for, 30–32
connections to learning and, 6
external rewards and, 30
relevance and, 31, 39
Mozart effect, 12
Mr. Holland's Opus, 99
multiple intelligences theory, 2, 22
music, classroom environment
and, 12

name game, 11
National Board Certification candidates, 14, 24, 121–22, 130
National Board Certified teachers, 25
New Basics, The: Education and the Future of Work in the Telematic Age (Thornburg), 39–40, 68
New York Sunday Times, 47
nonacademic skills, grading and, 87–88
norms, group, 22, 24
"Not Funnies" (McGrath), 47
"not yet ready for a grade," 26, 57

organization, classroom, 10, 14–15
Out of Our Minds (Robinson), 28
output, retention and, 4–5

pacing plans, 41–41
Palincsar, Ann-Marie, 108–9
Palmer, Parker, 9
paraphrasing, 122
parents
  behavior of, in student-led conferences, 92, 93
  communication with, 89
  final assessment by, 98
  inviting to student-led conferences, 92, 93
  involvement of, 97, 99
  letters to, 92, 93
  preparing for student-led conferences, 91–92
  student achievement and, 80
  student-led conferences and, 89–90
passages, celebrating, 27
passion, transferring to students, 127–28
patterns, 100
peer learning
  peer editing, 55–57
  read-arounds, 57–60
  value of, 131
picture books, 13
Pirsig, Robert M., 51
point of view, 45
portfolio-management systems, 65
portfolio reflection
  end-of-semester/end-of-year, 81, 82
  first reflection, 71–78
  Four-Week Reflection, 74
  second reflection, 79, 81
  Ten-Week Reflection, 80, 81
portfolios, 64–82
  advantages of, 65
  behavioral goals for, 70–72

clear, consistent, and convincing contents of, 68–69
evidence in, 69–70
handouts for, 66
improving, 96
instructional goals for, 66–69
manila folders for, 65–66
outcomes, 96
presentation of, in student-led conferences, 90
purposes of, 64
redemption through, 32
reflection and, 71–82
by teachers, 81
Pour Your Heart Into It (Schultz), 61
powerfulness, motivation and, 31
practice, 5
predictions
  in interactive reading, 111–12, 113–14, 115
  teaching how to make, 114
presentations
  for The Squeeze strategy, 116
  in student-led conferences, 90
print materials, in classroom, 12–13
prioritizing
  learning and, 2–3
  procrastination *vs.*, 86
proactivity, 85
procrastination, 86
productivity, portfolios and, 68
progress, gauging, 58
projects
  in KWL strategy, 107–8
  value of, 4–5
promotion, 81

questions. *See also* inquiry
  for assessment, 52–53
  effectiveness of, 129–30
  essential, 43–46
  in interactive reading, 110–12
  "known response," 48
  learning how to ask, 113
  not knowing answers to, 129
  for shared inquiry, 46–48
  student-generated, 48

rain gutters, as book shelves, 12
raising hands
  guidelines for, 17, 20
  wait time and, 5
read-arounds, 60–62

Index

139
∎

reading
    background knowledge and, 4
    learning and, 4
reading process, 108–9
Real Story of the 3 Little Pigs, The, 13
Reciprocal Teaching strategy. *See* interactive reading
Recorder, in The Squeeze strategy, 116
redemption, opportunities for, 32
reflection
    end-of-semester/end-of-year, 81, 82
    first reflection, for portfolios, 71–78
    on learning, 27–28
    in learning journals, 79
    modeling, 73, 76
    portfolios and, 71–82
    post-conference, 94, 96
    second reflection, for portfolios, 79–81
    Student Four-Week Reflection, 74–75
    Student Ten-Week Reflection, 80
    teacher feedback on, 76–78
    by teachers, 48–49, 62–63, 124–25
    value of, 28–29, 78, 87–88
Reflective Conversation Questions, 55
Reflective Conversation Questions and Statements strategy, 121–24
rehearsal, 5
relevance
    of instructional goals, 38–37
    learning and, 3
    motivation and, 31, 39
renewal, 87–88
repetition, by teachers, 84
respect, for students, 11
responsibility, student acceptance of, 76, 85
retention
    factors affecting, 3–4
    output and, 4–5
    teaching strategies and, 5–6
revision, 61
rewards, motivation and, 30
risk-taking
    classroom environment and, 127
    emotional safety and, 25
    in teaching, 42
Robinson, Ken, 28
Rosenbaum, James E., 87
routines, value of, 15
rules
    group norms, 22, 24
    questioning, 20

Salter, Chuck, 126
Say, in Say, Mean, Matter Strategy, 118
Say, Mean, Matter strategy, 118–20
    modeling, 119–20
    practicing, 119–20
scented candles, in classroom, 12
school districts, grading mandated by, 59
Schultz, Howard, 61–62, 126, 128
Schwartz, Peter, 39
Science standard (California State Framework), 45
scripting, for student-led conferences, 94, 95
seating arrangements, 11, 21
self-assessment
    sef-reported grading, 59–60
    value of, 58
self-organization, 45
self-reported grading, 59–60
    inflated, 75
    underreporting, 76–77
sentence starters, for learning communities, 122–24
7 Habits of Highly Effective Teens, The (Covey), 84–88
shared inquiry, 46–48
sheriff-for-the-day, 18
short-term memory, 3
sight, learning and, 2
silence, 20–21
    mindful, 86
slow learners, background knowledge and, 4
smell, in classroom, 12
Smilkstein, Rita, 1
social interaction, encouraging, 20–21
Socratic circles, 21
Socratic seminars, 85
sounds, in classroom, 12
Sousa, David A., 1, 5
Squeeze strategy, 116–18
    audience for, 116
    effectiveness of, 117–18
    preparation for, 116
    presentation, 117
    roles, 116
standardized tests, 42–43
standards
    assessment and, 52
    English Language Arts, 36
    grading and, 66–67
    instructional goals and, 34–35
    Math standards (California State Framework), 44

Science standard (California State Framework), 45
student demonstration of mastery over, 67–81
student-friendly version, 36–37
value of, 34–35
Student Four-Week Reflection, 74–75
student-led conferences, 89–99
assuring student and family attendance at, 92, 94
coordinating with other teachers, 90–91
improving, 96
inviting parents to, 92
listening to, 130–31
outcomes of, 96–97
parent assessment of, 98
parents and, 89–90
post-conference reflection, 94, 96
preparation for, 91–92
principles of, 90
scripting, 94, 95
ten-week reflection and, 80
year-end, 80, 97
student portfolios. See portfolios
Student Quiz: The Brain and Learning, 8
students
class rules created by, 22, 24
focusing on, 127
gauging progress of, 58
getting to know, 10–11, 127, 129
getting to know each other, 10–11
goal setting by, 85
inviting to learn, 18–19
learning names of, 10–11
responsibility of, 85
as Sheriff-for-the-day, 18
teacher beliefs and biases about, 13–14
as teachers, 6, 131
transferring passion to, 127–28
unteachable, 19
Student Ten-Week Reflection, 80, 81
Summarizer, in The Squeeze strategy, 116
summarizing
in interactive reading, 109, 113, 114
value of, 113
summative assessments, 53–54
Sutton, Shelia, 118
symbols, for Active Reading Symbols strategy, 121
synergy, 87

teachers
accountability of, 99
attitudes toward students, 31
attitudes toward teaching, 14
beliefs and biases of, 13–14
burn-out in, 125
getting to know students, 10–11
guidelines for, xiii–xv
importance of, ix
professional portfolios, 81
reflection by, 48–49, 62–63, 124–25
repetition by, 84
reputations of, 9
traits of, 126–32
writing binders, 13
teaching
effective, 126–32
risk-taking in, 42
by students, 6
teacher attitudes toward, 14
teaching strategies, 101–25
Active Reading Symbols, 120–21
classroom management and, ix
domesticating, 102–3
guidelines for using, 5–7, xiii–xv
interactive reading, 106–15
KWL (Know, Want to know, Learn) strategy, 7, 104–6
learning and, 5–7
liberating, 102–4
mindfulness and, xiii–xv
reflection on, 125
Reflective Conversation Questions and Statements, 121–24
Say, Mean, Matter, 118–20
The Squeeze, 116–18
value of, 101–2
test-taking strategies, 42–43
think column, in KWL strategy, 105
thinking
calorie consumption and, 2
encouraging, 5
Thornburg, David, 39–40, 68, 70
time, motivation and, 31
Toffler, Alvin, 83
touch, learning and, 2
twenty-four hour blast, 106

underachieving students
inflated self-reported grading by, 76–77
understanding relationship of efforts and result by, 77–78

Verifier, in The Squeeze strategy, 116
Vygotsky, Lev, 6

wait time, 5, 86
Wiggins, Grant, 37
win-win attitude, 26, 86
Wisconsin, University of, 42
Wolk, S., 22
wonder column, in KWL strategy, 105
Works Cited pages, 108
writing binders, teacher's, 13
Wyatt, R. L., III, 64

year-end student-led conferences, 81, 97

Zone of Proximal Development, 6